CROSS COUNTRY SKIER'S TRAILSIDE GUIDE

CROSS COUNTRY SKIER'S TRAILSIDE GUIDE

By Craig Woods And Gordon Hardy
With The Editors Of CROSS COUNTRY SKIER Magazine

Illustrated By Austin Stevens

The Stephen Greene Press
Brattleboro, Vermont
Lexington, Massachusetts

Credits: Cover photograph by David Madison. All inside photographs by Cook Neilson. Wax chart on the back cover appears courtesy of Swix Sport USA, Incorporated. The editors would like to thank Eric Evans, Jim Johnson, and Glenn Jobe for their help in preparing this book.

First Edition

This book is manufactured in the United States of America. It is designed by Ken Silvia Design Group and published by The Stephen Greene Press, Fessenden Road, Brattleboro, Vermont 05301.

3/87 Gift

Library of Congress Cataloging in Publication Data

Main entry under title:

Cross country skier's trailside guide.

Includes index.
1. Cross-country skiing—Handbooks, manuals, etc.
I. Cross country skier. II. Title: Trailside guide.
GV855.3.C77   1983   796.93   83–11658
ISBN 0-8289-0512-6 (pbk.)

For Kate and Aster

CONTENTS

WELCOME TO
CROSS COUNTRY SKIING!

T he *Trailside Guide* is a ready reference you can slip into a pocket or pack to answer questions that arise on the trail. It concentrates on general touring and light touring—that is, the kind of skiing you will be doing at developed touring centers and on day tours to off-track areas, such as parks, golf courses, and public lands.

The *Trailside Guide* also deals with getting ready to ski, with conditioning, equipment and clothing selection, and planning a tour. This is because unprepared frequently means unenjoyable when you get your skis onto the snow. Once you're on the snow the *Trailside Guide* becomes your companion, there to answer questions about wax selection, ski technique, safety, trailside etiquette, and other topics.

This is not a survival manual for ski mountaineering nor an emergency handbook for winter-camping enthusiasts. These disciplines have their own body of first-rate literature. This is a book for recreational day tourers.

Even at a sophisticated touring center you'll find moments when questions about waxing or basic technique or etiquette occur and you're on your own to answer them. And sooner or later, if you are to progress in skiing, you'll have to answer these questions yourself. Toward gaining self-reliance—a key to proficiency in any endeavor—we hope the *Trailside Guide* helps you build a strong foundation.

Happy skiing!

CHAPTER ONE

EQUIPMENT

T he proper selection of ski equipment is essential to enjoying cross country skiing and to becoming a better skier. A universal attraction of cross country is the simplicity of gear required, and even in this day of higher and higher technology, simplicity remains the watchword in this sport.

In this chapter we will present an overview of cross country ski equipment. When you learn in a generic way the function and important characteristics of each piece of equipment, you can apply it to the specific choices you'll face in a ski shop—whether purchasing your first pair of skis or "trading up" to equipment that better complements a higher skill level you've attained.

"Complement" is an important word here, for the right ski equipment must not only complement your skiing ability, it is comprised of components that must complement each other. And all of your gear, in turn, must complement the kind of skiing you will be doing.

A beginning skier, for example, who plans to spend three or four weekends a winter skiing on golf courses near home will be best off with touring or light-touring skis that are relatively wide. This will provide the stability the beginner appreciates. Waxless skis are a good idea to eliminate the problem of correct wax selection, which can be a stumbling block for beginners. Sturdy bindings matched to medium-weight, medium-height boots are also recommended. The outfit may be rounded out with fiberglass or aluminum poles. This gear will not cost a lot (probably under $150.00) and it will give the skier a reliable outfit. The beginner won't feel as though he has to love skiing because he's spent so much money on it, and he won't be impeded by equipment designed for skilled skiers.

On the other hand, the advanced skier is looking for lighter boots, bindings, and poles, and lighter and narrower skis to help him go faster. His technique is polished, and he can make this gear work properly for him. He already knows that he likes the sport enough to spend the money on this more expensive outfit. He probably likes to ski on groomed trails in set tracks. If he wants also to spend a lot of time on ungroomed terrain, he will likely invest in a second, sturdier outfit for that purpose.

One word of caution when you are considering a purchase: Inexpensive doesn't have to mean cheap, and expensive doesn't always mean high quality. Take some time to do your homework before spending your money—books such as this, magazine articles, and qualified ski-shop personnel are invaluable when you're closing in on a purchase, especially when brand familiarity becomes a factor. There is so much high-quality ski equipment available at all ability levels and price levels that no skier should end up without reliable, high-quality gear that fits his pocketbook.

SKIS

The ski, of course, is the key ingredient. Cross country skis are long, thin, beautiful things, and today's models are products of sophisticated designs from research and development by major companies. There are specialized skis for racing, in-track touring, backcountry touring, and other types of skiing. Following are characteristics of cross country skis you should consider in order to select the pair of skis that complements your ability level and the kind of skiing you'll be doing.

MATERIALS. Until recent years, cross country skis were made entirely of wood. Many of these skis had hardened wood edges and a wood base that needed to be waxed to provide the correct grip and glide for cross country skiing. All-wood skis are still available from a handful of manufacturers, but they are well on their way out. Most of today's skis are made from fiberglass combined with other synthetics (wood is used in some fiberglass models as a ski-core component).

The advantages of fiberglass over wood are several. Fiberglass skis are more durable. The synthetic base materials allow effective waxless construction. In waxable versions, these bases are

Examples of cross country ski bases. The two bases at left are waxable synthetic bases (note metal edges on base at extreme left). Center is a waxless patterned base. Second from right is a waxless insert base. At extreme right is a wood base.

easier to wax and they glide better than wood. Fiberglass skis are also lighter than wood skis. And, finally, when compared to wood skis, fiberglass models are almost maintenance free.

In sophisticated racing models, manufacturers have introduced synthetics that have further advantages over fiberglass. Such materials as graphite (also called carbon-fiber) and Kevlar appear in the construction of some skis, and, as is the case with many such innovations, these materials are beginning to filter down to the recreational level.

Some skis designed for use in deep snow and in backcountry touring that involves a lot of downhill runs are produced with metal edges. Like the metal edges on alpine skis, these are designed to help carve turns. Some very specialized cross country skis are produced for use on groomed downhill slopes—with the skiers riding lifts up and skiing down—and these are referred to as telemarking skis.

WAXABLE OR WAXLESS? This is a question that is becoming increasingly hard for all skiers to answer. The first waxless skis appeared only a few years ago, and while their performance was good, it could not compare to the performance of a well-waxed ski. Now, each year brings new waxless skis that perform better and better.

The concept behind a waxless construction is simple. All cross country skis are built with camber (or a slight bow) under the foot section. When you step off or kick off with one foot, it collapses the camber to push the ski base against the snow. To gain purchase in order to push yourself forward, your ski base must grip the snow. That's where the wax comes in—it grips against the tiny crystals of the snow. If you take a ski base and do something to it that allows it to grip without using wax, you've created a waxless ski.

Early waxless designs involved creating a pattern in the base that would grip when pushed against the snow. But the pattern was also such that when the ski moved forward, it didn't interfere appreciably with glide. This is known as a patterned waxless base, and refined versions are available on many current models. Other early waxless skis used synthetic mohair; the tiny hairs created resistance when pushed in one direction (back, as during kick) and laid flat when pushed in the other (forward, as during glide).

Recent waxless designs have incorporated synthetic base inserts under the foot area that provide grip without hindering glide. Some of these new waxless inserts work "chemically"—no fooling!—with the snow, using the hydrophilic quality of the insert to do so. Hydrophilic means water-attracting, and under correct conditions, a hydrophilic material can create just the grip needed to propel a skier forward. Other waxless designs are variations of the patterned-base approach (or "mechanical" approach), using such materials for grip as mica chips and tiny polypropylene hairs. The mica chips or synthetic hairs are aligned to slide when the ski moves forward but to grip when the ski is pushed backward as you kick.

There are skis that combine the properties of waxable and waxless in one base—informally called "waxable waxless" skis. Perhaps in acknowledgment of the failure of most waxless bases in certain snow conditions, these bases are designed so they can be waxed if grip is poor.

Patterned waxless bases and waxable waxless bases from reputable manufacturers are the only waxless skis that have proven consistently effective under a wide range of snow conditions at this writing. But waxless innovations are coming so fast and furiously that even better waxless skis may soon be available; it is unfortunately impossible to foresee what may be on the market in the future and how well it will work, even for this season. Magazine articles, advertisements, and ski-shop personnel will help you keep abreast of new developments in the marketplace.

The obvious advantage to waxless skis is that you don't have to wax them. Just grab the skis, clip your boots into the bindings, and go! And you won't have to clean wax off your skis when you return. The not-so-obvious disadvantage to waxless skis is that the base doesn't work equally well in all snow conditions, and you can't adjust the waxless base as you can adjust the wax on a pair of waxable skis. Some skiers will also tell you that waxless skis interfere with glide and that nothing can ever compare to skiing on a well-waxed ski. A characteristic of some pattern-based waxless skis pointed to as a disadvantage is that they can be noisy—the waxless pattern makes a buzzing sound during glide.

Since waxing skis can be difficult, and impossible for people without the patience for something that may require trial and error, waxless skis have their place for the beginner and for the casual skier who would just as soon enjoy the advantage of less time preparing for an outing. Many parents, who may themselves be expert waxers and skiers, swear by waxless skis for family outings. It seems the pleasure of waxing diminishes somewhat when you must wax your own skis and the children's skis as well. Some skiers have skis they wax and another waxless pair—the waxless skis they use when they want to skip out quickly for a tour or when the snow conditions are such that they figure even the best wax job they can produce is not going to work very well.

Many skiers who are just getting into cross country begin on waxless skis, and when they feel they can ski well enough to enjoy the benefits of a waxable ski, they trade in their waxless skis for a waxable pair or simply add a waxable pair to their gear.

LENGTH. The traditional method for finding the right length of ski is to measure it against your upward reach. Standing with your arm raised straight up, the ski should reach your wrist.

This is obviously a simplified method of judging correct ski length—but it works pretty well. Many models of skis today are produced with varying stiffnesses, which argues against the simple reach-up test. Since the multiplicity of models available makes it impossible to devise a foolproof standard test, the best advice is to find out if the ski in question has an especially stiff or soft overall flex that would preclude a useful reach-up test—if not, reach away. A simple guide here is to bear in mind that ski length is combined with a stiffness for the height of the average skier who will be using the ski. So if you're light for your height, you will want either a shorter ski (that will have a softer flex) or a softer flex built into the longer ski. The reverse is true for skiers who are heavy for their height.

SHAPE. The shape of a ski refers to the relationship of its dimensions at tip, waist, and tail. A javelin ski is narrower at the tip than it is at the waist. The javelin shape is used almost exclusively for cross country racing in well-maintained tracks. It does not turn well and it does not float well in out-of-track snow. A parallel ski is the same width from behind the tip to the tail. A parallel ski, like the javelin ski, is primarily for in-track skiing and racing. A sidecut ski has a waist that is narrower than tip or tail. This hourglass shape suits a ski best for turning and off-track skiing when the amount of sidecut is great. The sidecut ski from a gentle sidecut through a dramatic sidecut, is the overwhelming preference of skiers from set-track enthusiasts to cross country downhillers.

WIDTH. The narrower the ski the more it is intended for going fast—and the greater skill it requires to make it perform. Thus, the very narrow skis (with waists of 44 to 48 millimeters) are racing and high-performance light-touring models. For general touring and most touring-center skiing, a novice or intermediate will want a sidecut ski that is about 48 to 55 millimeters wide at the waist. This offers a good combination between stability, skill demand on the skier, and performance capability.

FLEX. A cross country ski is built with camber—a slight bow or arching underneath the boot and binding area. When you take a step or stride, you weight this area, which presses it down onto the snow to gain grip from your wax or waxless base. When you glide, you glide primarily on the tip and tail areas and the arch returns somewhat to the ski.

The area that you bring in contact with the snow is called the wax pocket. And the measure of overall flex in a ski is how much force it takes to press the wax pocket onto the snow.

Generally speaking, strong, skillful skiers prefer a stiff ski because they can use their strength and skill to kick at the perfect time to bring the wax pocket most efficiently in contact with the snow. The stiff ski rebounds quickly to help the glide phase. Skier weight comes into play here, too. The heavier the skier the stiffer the ski should be.

The best way to find out if the flex of a ski suits you is to try out that model of ski. If you're unable to field test the ski, there is a simple test that will tell you if a ski has sufficient stiffness for you. Place both skis on the floor and stand on them in the spot where the boots will be. If another person can run a piece of paper underneath the area in which the wax pocket should be, the ski is stiff enough for your weight. The wax pocket should run about one foot fore and six inches aft of the ball of your foot (about 18 inches in all). If there is enough room between the ski and the floor to slip a piece of cardboard or several sheets of paper through—then the ski is probably too stiff for you. If there is no space to slip anything under the ski, it is too soft. Now, put all your weight on one ski. Can you pin the paper to the floor? If so, the ski is the right flex for you. This is not very scientific, but fortunately for most of us this is not an area of fine tuning—and skiing, after all, is an inexact science. Also, a fairly wide general-touring ski or a light-touring ski with moderate sidecut will have a flex to match up with the length of the ski and the kind of skier for whom it is designed.

BOOTS

A lot is asked of good cross country ski boots. They must keep your feet warm and dry. They must be comfortable while flexing in the correct place to allow you to stride. They must be light to make skiing easy. They must be durable. And they must have a sole with enough lateral stability to transmit the force of your kick to the ski with little wasted side-to-side motion. Below are the important features of a ski boot and how they work to satisfy these requirements.

HEIGHT AND WEIGHT. The height of a boot is important in keeping your feet warm and dry. Height does not appreciably affect the lateral stability of the boot. The trade-off is in weight,

Cross country boots and bindings come in styles to complement all skiing situations. At left is Salomon's touring boot with compatible Salomon Nordic System (SNS) binding. The Adidas boot (second from left) matches with a special binding and is designed for light touring. The center boot is an Alfa light-touring model that fits a 50-millimeter binding. Dynafit's LIN system (second from right) is designed for light touring and racing. At extreme right is a Norrona backcountry boot for a 75-millimeter binding.

for a higher boot is heavier than a lower boot. Racers choose boots cut below the ankle for lightness and speed; because they work vigorously, racers generate heat to keep their feet warm enough in low boots. Light tourers and tourers choose boots cut at ankle height or just above the ankle. The extra height helps keep deep snow out of the boot. And because they are not working as hard as racers, the extra height also retains more heat. The highest and sturdiest boots are worn by backcountry skiers to whom the safety of warmth, dryness, and durability is decidedly more important than lightness.

FLEX. A cross country boot must flex comfortably in the sole at the ball of the foot. If it does not, you won't be able to stride forward and kick off with your foot. To check this you can flex the sole of a boot manually or put the boots on and judge how they flex on your feet according to how they must flex on your skis.

LATERAL STABILITY. Lateral stability helps you kick efficiently without wasteful side-to-side movement. High-quality cross country boots incorporate this feature into the design of the boot, but you can get an idea of how much stability is in a boot by twisting it on a lateral axis that simulates the side-to-side pressure you apply with your foot when skiing. The stiffer a boot is on this axis, the better.

CONSTRUCTION. Boots are available with leather or synthetic uppers mated to hard-rubber or synthetic soles. Leather, though heavier than synthetics, is likely to be warmer. Some synthetics, nylon primarily, are used exclusively for lightness in racing boots at the expense of warmth. Other synthetics are now being used that are warm, breathable, and light, and the best known of these is Gore-Tex. Such synthetics are also waterproof—except where sewn-through seams are exposed. When considering a boot with such an upper, find out if the seams are sewn through, and—if they are—what added feature prevents water from getting in there.

Other features of boots, such as lining, should be taken into consideration on a personal basis. If you plan to wear two pairs of socks and generally don't feel cold discomfort in your feet, a heavy lining may be unnecessary for you.

Purchase of a leather boot means that you will have to take care of it as you would any leather footwear. Leather-conditioning and waterproofing products that contain silicon are recommended. And if you rub some of the silicon on the boot sole and the ski's binding plate it will help prevent troublesome snow and ice build-up in these areas while skiing.

BINDING COMPATIBILITY. The sole of a cross country boot is made at the toe so that it can be clipped into a binding. There are now a number of binding types available, each one of which accommodates a specific sole design. Two or three pins in the binding fit into corresponding holes in the sole toe, and in some cases no pins are used. Make sure that the boot you select is made to fit the binding you plan to use.

BINDINGS

There have been many changes in recent years in the cross country binding, all of which have been aimed at making the critical connection between boot and ski as efficient as possible. This has resulted in an increased number of binding types on the market, which can be broken down into three categories: the Nordic norms, the 50-millimeter systems, and the special systems.

The Nordic norms include bindings that are 71, 75, and 79 millimeters wide (across the three pins on the plate). These norms were established to simplify binding and boot compatibility in the marketplace. A boot for one of these bindings has a sole designated with a corresponding 71-, 75-, or 79-millimeter width. The 75-millimeter-wide binding has been the standard choice of light-touring and general-touring skiers. It is reliable, inexpensive, and a wide range of boot models are made to fit this binding. The 71- and 79-millimeter-wide bindings were initially designed for racing and off-track skiing respectively, but the versatility of the 75 and the introduction of new racing bindings have rendered these norms all but obsolete.

The 50-millimeter systems include the 50-7 and the 50-12 bindings (the seven and the 12 refer to the thickness in millimeters of the compatible boot sole). The 50-millimeter-wide binding was originally designed for racers—being narrower than the Nordic norm bindings, it does not interfere with the sidewalls of the set tracks of a race course. When adapted for use by other in-track, light-touring skiers, these skiers found their feet got too cold because the sole of the boot that fit this binding was just seven millimeters thick. So a binding was developed for boots with 12-millimeter-thick soles for added warmth, and thus the two 50-millimeter models available today, the 50-7 and 50-12.

The special systems are the newest bindings, with different models available from Salomon (called the Salomon Nordic System, or SNS), Trak, Adidas, Nike, and Dynafit (called the LIN system). Though these bindings were originally and are still to a degree associated with racing, they are suitable also for light-touring and beginning skiers. Because of the patenting of some of the new systems, you must buy a compatible boot from the binding manufacturer (or one of its licensees), but a wide range of boots is available from these manufacturers to answer the needs of general and light tourers at various skill levels.

Your choice of binding system—Nordic norm, 50-millimeter, or one of the special systems—is your own to make, for they all work well. The new special systems are frequently called "integrated boot/binding systems," but as you can see all boot/binding relationships are integrated systems. Because all of the

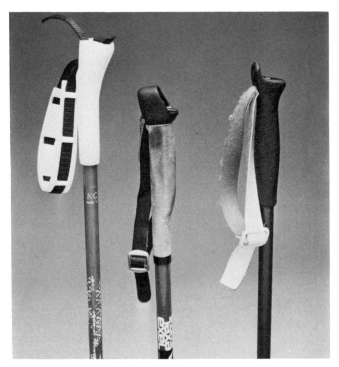

Common pole-strap and handle styles. Each of these models is "ambidextrous" (can be used with either right or left hand) and features an adjustable strap.

systems available perform the most important function of a binding—the efficient transmission of force to the ski—the question becomes which system suits your skiing. In the new special systems the light-touring skier can benefit from features that help extend the kick phase and from the narrowness that doesn't interfere with a set track's sidewall.

POLES
Here is your easiest equipment choice. There are only a few points to keep in mind when selecting a pole.

Poles are available in tonkin cane (bamboo), fiberglass, metal, and lightweight synthetics. The latter poles, which are

Ski-pole baskets that are smallest, such as those at extreme right and left, are designed for light touring or racing—that is, skiing where a pole track has been set. The second basket from left is a standard touring model, and the second basket from right is full and round for backcountry use in deep powder. Note that the pole points are designed to release easily when you pick up for a plant.

made from such materials as boron and graphite, are essentially for racers, due to the high strength-per-weight ratio found in such materials. The light and general tourer, however, is better off with a less expensive pole made from one of the other materials. Fiberglass or metal is probably the best bet, as either material makes a light, durable, and inexpensive pole. Bamboo poles are the least expensive, but they are also the easiest to break.

Features to look for in a pole beyond shaft construction include strap characteristics and tip and basket type. Some straps are adjustable. An adjustable strap allows you to maintain a comfortable grasp and to make the strap longer or shorter according to the bulkiness of the gloves or mittens you are wearing. Some straps are also "ambidextrous"—that is, the right- and left-hand straps come off the handle the same way. If the pole strap is not ambidextrous, note that the part of the strap that comes off the top of the grip should be on the outside, and your thumb should go over the part of the strap that comes off lower on the handle. Make sure the poles you buy, if not ambidextrous, include a right- and left-hand model.

A good cross country pole also has a tip (point) that points forward. This enables the tip to come out of the snow easily as you bring the pole up for another plant.

There are a variety of basket shapes available. Smaller baskets (some are half-moon shaped, for instance) are designed for racing and skiing on well-groomed trails. A full, round basket is recommended for the light and general tourer. Back-country skiers often opt for oversize baskets that do not penetrate too deeply into unpacked powder snow.

To choose the correct length of pole, stand on the floor in your stocking feet. The top of the pole's handle should just reach your armpit.

BASE PREPARATION

Fresh off the rack, a new ski looks ready to go. Most man-ufacturers, however, recommend that you prepare the ski base—whether waxable or waxless—before use. There are different procedures here for skis with synthetic bases and for skis with wood bases.

SYNTHETIC BASES. In most cases, if you examine the base of a new plastic-base ski you'll see tiny hairs of whitish-colored plastic along the running surface. For the best skiing, these should be removed and the entire base smoothed to an even finish before use. To do this, lock the ski base in a vise or stabilize it at an angle from the floor

Most new ski bases can use a moment of preparation before ski-ing. On synthetic bases, scrape carefully with a metal scraper.

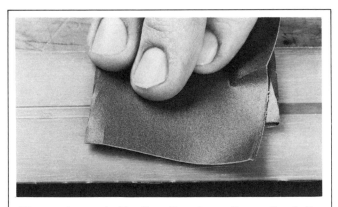

After scraping, sand with a fine-grit sandpaper. You can then buff the sanded surface with a waxing cork and apply binder and glide waxes (see Chapter Five).

to the workbench. Set the edge of a metal wax scraper or furniture scraper flat against the base and scrape down, always moving from tip to tail. Work carefully; a metal scraper is far more likely than a plastic one to gouge the base if you slip, but a plastic scraper won't smooth the base sufficiently (make sure the edge of your metal scraper

Wood bases need a bit more preparation than synthetic bases. Pine tar is a standby choice for waterproofing the base. After scraping and sanding as with synthetic bases, heat the sticky pine tar with a few passes of a torch.

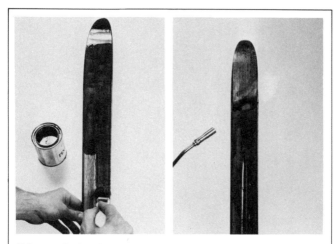

Using a paint brush, apply the pine tar liberally to the base. Heat the pine tar with a few passes of the propane torch to liquefy it, making it easier to wipe off.

is sharp). Try to keep an even pressure along the width of the ski. Don't use too much force; a few extra passes with the scraper are better than too much force that results in a gouge. When the base is smooth, sand it with very fine (220- to 400-grade) sandpaper, then buff with a rag or waxing cork. You may also heat in paraffin wax on the glide sections of the ski. Scrape and buff the paraffin to a barely visible layer before applying glide wax. (Methods of heating in wax are covered in Chapter Five.)

Waxless bases are also synthetic, but require less preparation. Scrape down, sand, and polish the running surfaces (tip and tail, in front of and behind the base pattern or waxless insert) of the ski in the method described above. Preparation of the pattern in a pattern-base waxless model is usually unnecessary—you don't want to sand it down, and most irregularities will be eliminated by a few kilometers of skiing. You may also want to rub down the tips and tails with a special waxless ski glide formula such as Maxiglide. This is a slippery solution that increases the glide potential of the base without interfering with the performance of the waxless pattern or base insert.

WOOD BASES. Wood bases require more preparation

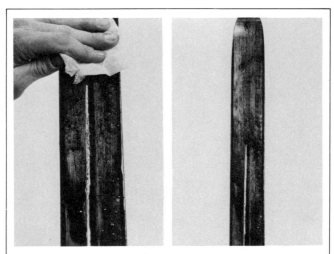

Wipe the liquefied pine tar off with a rag or a piece of fiberlene. The treated ski base should have a rich, nut-brown finish. When the entire base has been treated, let sit overnight.

than plastic bases. They must be rendered waterproof, or moisture will seep in and warp or delaminate the ski. Pine tar is the preferred waterproofing agent. Pine tar is a very thick, sticky concoction that is available in cans.

Set the ski base in a vise or secure it at an angle to the floor. Scrape the ski down with a wax scraper and sand with fine sandpaper until the base is smooth and any varnish that may have been applied at manufacture for preskiing protection is removed. Once the base is smooth, light a propane torch and pass the flame across your can of pine tar a few times. This will warm the tar, liquifying it to a greater degree to make application to the ski base easier. When the tar is warm and runny, paint a thick coat over the entire ski base with a paintbrush.

Once applied, the pine tar must be worked into the wood. Pass the torch over a section of the base—not letting it stay so long in one spot that it burns the base but long enough for the tar to start bubbling. Then wipe off the excess tar with a rag. What should remain is a smooth, nut-brown base. After treating the full length of the base in this manner, allow to sit overnight, then apply paraffin and glide wax as described above.

CHAPTER TWO

CLOTHING

D ressing for cross country skiing is a matter of keeping warm and dry. This is not as simple as it sounds, due to the active nature of the sport. In downhill skiing, for example, the primary needs in clothing are insulation and protection from the elements. But cross country clothing must not only insulate and protect, it must also vent away excess heat and wick away excess moisture from the body. Cross country skiing is an active sport in which you may generate a lot of body heat and perspiration. If excess heat and perspiration are not handled properly by the clothing you choose, they will make you wet and uncomfortable.

The way to handle this is to create a clothing system that vents, wicks, insulates, and protects from the elements at the same time. And you also want your body's reactions to be complemented by easy and convenient adjustments you can make to your system. This is because the weather can turn colder or warmer, and because, for example, after exercising vigorously to get up a hill you may take a break but want to avoid cooling off too rapidly. Sound like a tall order to fill? It is—but with the aid of modern fabric technology and the development of clothing styles specifically for cross country skiers, the order is easily filled.

The system we are talking about is based on the layering principle in dressing, using three layers, and it works like this: You choose a first layer of clothing to wear next to your body that incorporates wicking and breathing properties to transmit excess heat and moisture away from your skin. You choose a second layer of clothing that absorbs the wicked-away moisture and insulates at the same time. You choose a third layer of clothing that protects you from the elements. And that's the system!

Let's look at the kinds of garments that make up these layers.

LAYER ONE: UNDERWEAR

The best underwear for active winter sports such as cross country skiing is made from polypropylene. This synthetic, when combined with other materials, makes a garment that wicks moisture away from the skin into the next layer of clothing, keeping your skin dry. Polypropylene underwear is now available from several companies in tops and bottoms. It is light, comfortable, and—if it matters to you—it is available in a variety of colors and patterns.

Other forms of underwear are also available, and though they are not as specifically functional for cross country as polypropylene, they can do the job. Such garments are cotton and wool long and regular underwear. A difference here is that these materials tend to absorb moisture. If you are not going to work hard enough to perspire a great deal, there is nothing wrong with the wool- and cotton-content underwear.

Some specialized cross country bottoms are available with wind-resistant crotch areas in models for men and women to guard against frostbite and discomfort there.

LAYER TWO: ABSORPTION AND INSULATION

Both of these properties can be found in a variety of garments in a variety of materials. This absorbing and insulating layer can actually be made up of many layers to be shed and replaced as the weather dictates. Insulation and warmth is provided by air that is heated by your body and trapped within these layers. So, when you choose clothing for this layer, the more separate garments you have the greater your ability to fine tune your system—to adjust to changing conditions and body temperature.

Turtlenecks and shirts with a wool makeup are good absorbing layers. Cotton garments, unlike wool, have little insulating value when wet. A turtleneck is a good choice to go over the underwear layer to absorb moisture, and it will help retain heat because the high collar keeps in heat that otherwise would be vented away quickly.

Many garments are available whose function is primarily to insulate. Worn over the turtleneck, they are more for heat retention than moisture absorption. Two standout materials for this layer are wool and pile in the form of sweaters and zip-front vests and jackets. Wool and pile are standouts not only for their insulation value, but also because if they are called upon to insulate when wet (due to perspiration from inside or precipitation from outside) they can do it. Another form of insulation is down, but it does not insulate when wet, and when dry it can insulate too much for cross country skiing. But both wool and pile incorporate some breathing properties that aid in venting excess heat, and the zip-front pile or wool vest or jacket is a very good choice, for the zipper can be opened for further venting.

Socks, pants, hats, and gloves can be considered under the insulation category. Heavy wool socks are the best choice for comfort, insulation, and absorption, and a pair worn over lighter nylon, polypropylene, or wool undersocks usually does the trick.

Long wool pants or wool knickers are adequate under most conditions. Lightweight knickers made from poplin are also good, and there are now even corduroy knickers made specifically for cross country. The corduroy is treated to be water resistant—the major problem with previous corduroys. The traditional knicker style is associated with cross country clothing so closely for very good reasons: The style is comfortable during active exercise and there is no pant cuff to become wet, frozen, and encumbering. Because venting, wicking, and insulating are not as critical here as in garments that cover the upper body, the knicker or a pair of long pants usually completes this part of the system.

The glove is an important choice in cross country, for it must provide, usually in a single garment, venting, wicking, insulation, and outer protection. And at the same time it should be supple enough to allow comfortable handling of the ski pole. As a result, you should look for gloves made specifically for cross country. Often these gloves incorporate a leather face and back attached to a wool inner glove. Synthetic materials such as Gore-Tex are now being used in gloves, for these materials incorporate insulating properties with protection, venting, and suppleness. Mittens are warmer than gloves, and if you don't mind sacrificing the extra dexterity that gloves allow in handling the ski pole, mittens are a good choice. You can use plain wool mittens, or, for very cold conditions a wool inner mitten can be covered by a leather or nylon outer mitten.

Most skiers find that an all-wool hat is too warm and creates excess perspiration that the wool absorbs. Cross country hats, then, shouldn't be confused with the heavy alpine ski hats—they should be lighter, should contain less wool in the makeup, and might even have a special band to absorb sweat. The pure wool hat, however, is excellent to have along in your pack to put on when you take a break and cooling down too quickly becomes the problem. Headbands that cover the forehead and ears are sometimes all you need, and these can help absorb perspiration to keep it out of your eyes. When in doubt about what kind of headgear to take on a tour, take more than you think you need, for hats are easy to store in a pack and to change as the conditions or your body requires.

For greater protection in the head area you can wear a balaclava, which is a hat that can be pulled down over your face with holes for your eyes and mouth. This keeps you warm and protects you from frostbite in severe cold. Balaclavas come in several materials, including wool, polypropylene, and silk.

LAYER THREE: OUTER PROTECTION

On the outside of your outfit you will want to choose clothing to protect you from wind and precipitation. Tightly knit un-lined shells fall into this category as do one- and two-piece cross country suits and heavily lined parkas—your choice, of course, depends on the conditions.

The lightweight water- and wind-resistant shells today are designed by many manufacturers specifically for cross country—that is, they have ample space in the arm and body areas to allow active movement. These are very light and may come in the form of pullovers or zip-front jackets. Again, a zip-front jacket has the advantage of being able to be opened to vent excess heat. On a day tour when you expect the weather to allow skiing with two layers—your outer layer being, perhaps, a sweater—it is an easy chore to fold up a pullover shell and stick it in your pack for insurance should the weather turn suddenly brisk. Also, if you face a long downhill stretch—where you will not be working hard (or at all) to create heat and where the wind will be in your face—you can slip a shell on over your sweater for comfort.

One- and two-piece cross country suits are frequently worn as the outer layer. Because they are manufactured to stretch comfortably when you ski and to fit tightly to diminish wind resistance they can offer neither a great deal of insulation nor protection from wind and precipitation. These suits are made for skiers who will be working hard to go fast, usually when skiing close to the lodges at developed touring centers, and so the need to handle changing conditions is not great. However, a light shell or another outer garment, such as a warm-up suit, is frequently worn over these suits for added warmth when the skier is not off and running full blast. These suits come in separate bottom and top combinations, one-piece full-length styles, and one-piece bib styles—all bottoms available as full-length pants or knickers.

Parkas, ranging from lightly insulated to heavily insulated models, offer the most protection from wind and precipitation. Down-insulated parkas are not a good choice here for the same reason down garments are not recommended for the insulating layer: Down doesn't insulate when wet. However, the outdoor-clothing market now features garments incorporating modern fabrics, such as Gore-Tex for outer protection and Thinsulate for insulation, that offer excellent insulation when dry or wet as well as wind resistance and water repellency. The Gore-Tex fabric also breathes while providing this protection. A hood on your parka provides an extra measure of protection when needed, as does a high, zip-up collar. Again, as in the light shell pullovers and jackets, parkas are available with the roominess needed to ski comfortably.

Gaiters can be worn over your boots and lower legs to protect from snow and wetness. They are made of water-repellent fabric and are available in ankle, mid-calf, and knee length. For extreme conditions, some gaiters are insulated.

Finally, a wind suit, which can be conveniently folded up and stored in your pack, is a good idea. You may have adequate insulation from all your layers but need simple wind and precipitation protection, and with little extra weight and insulation, a wind suit—in pants and tops—may be just the thing when a storm blows in or you find it's windier out than you thought.

CHAPTER THREE

SHAPING UP

C ross country skiing is superb exercise. Few other sports offer as complete a workout under such safe conditions. Whether you ski competitively or as part of a year-round exercise program or just for fun, your body will benefit from the exercise cross country offers. At any level of participation, skiing builds endurance, strength, and general well-being.

In most touring situations, cross country is aerobic exercise. Aerobic means "with oxygen." Fuel and oxygen are combined within the cells of the body to produce energy used in such exercise. It is distinguished from anaerobic exercise ("without oxygen"), in which the body quickly produces energy for short, sharp bursts of exertion, such as sprinting up a hill, which radically depletes oxygen stores. Since aerobic activity uses large amounts of oxygen over a sustained period, oxygen replenishment takes place, and this requires exercising more than just muscles; exercise of the respiratory and circulatory systems is also associated with aerobic exercise.

Aerobic exercise is best for overall fitness, and among various aerobic activities, cross country skiing places among the most complete and beneficial in laboratory tests. Just how much skiing is going to improve your health varies from individual to individual. But the classic measure of the midrange of aerobic exertion works for most everyone: If you can carry on a conversation while skiing steadily, you are engaged in moderate aerobic exercise.

But, like any aerobic workout, cross country requires a bit of preparation. Desk jobs, rich food, and lack of exercise are common among many people, and if it's been a while since you've run 10 kilometers or spent an hour on the soccer field, remember that you must work up to a good workout.

Shaping up is a matter of preparation and prevention. Stretching before a day tour warms up the muscles and prevents stiffness and possible stress injuries. Preseason training readies your muscles and increases cardiopulmonary (heart/lung) fitness. Both constitute a small investment of time for a worthwhile payback. In this chapter we'll suggest appropriate preseason activities and outline a program of stretching to help you prepare properly for a day's outing.

PRESEASON TRAINING

Preseason training prepares your body for the specific needs of cross country skiing. Cross country exercises virtually all your muscles, but legs, arms, and back are of particular importance. So are your lungs, which must adapt to winter's cold air and added energy requirements. Above all, you must exercise that most important of muscles, the heart.

Any exercise you enjoy will aid in your preseason training. Tennis, soccer, swimming, basketball, and other sports improve and maintain fitness and coordination. The most important aspect of training is that you do it regularly. If you exercise vigorously at least three times a week (reaching a pulse rate of 130 to 160 beats per minute for a minimum of 15 minutes) you should be able to maintain a standard of fitness that will serve you well come wintertime.

First, a word of caution. Start slowly, and don't expect aerobic miracles on the first day. If you aren't in good shape, or are 35 years old or older, consult your physician before beginning any conditioning program. And remember to choose an activity or exercise regimen that you'll stick with. The best training program in the world won't help you if you lose interest and give up on it. Below are some popular activities that help develop muscles for cross country's specific demands.

JOGGING AND RUNNING. Jogging is one of the most popular preseason workouts. The basic motion is almost identical to the diagonal stride of cross country. Additionally, it dovetails nicely with skiing in a program of year-round fitness. If you're already a serious runner, you've probably considered skiing as a good winter substitute, which it is. But unlike running, it avoids the jarring heel strike, giving your knees a four-month break from the rigors of the road.

You can imitate the motion of skiing if you run or even walk quickly with ski poles, and thereby build the specific muscles that will be used when skiing. Use the poles as you would when skiing. If you are running, run with your normal stride, keeping your weight forward and your shoulders level. If you are "ski-walking," elongate your stride to imitate the longer stride of cross country. Push off with your "kicking" leg as soon as the opposite pole touches the ground. Running and walking with poles is especially useful on hills; the naturally shortened stride imitates the short stride of skiing uphill.

HIKING. While not specific to cross country skiing, hiking is excellent exercise for your legs and back. Try to hike at a steady, fairly rapid pace, and maintain that pace when hiking uphill. As with running, ski poles will help you imitate the motion of cross country. Remove the baskets of your poles so they don't get tangled up in roots and rocks. If you can, use an old pair of poles, as they will probably get beat up with regular hiking. Keep your weight forward, and stride in as straight a line as you can manage on the trail.

BICYCLING. Bicycling is one of the most popular off-season activities for cross country skiers. Fully two-thirds of all skiers bicycle in the summer. This activity is, of course, especially useful for leg development. It also has the advantage of being an interesting and easily varied pastime. Try to work a regular bicycling program into your schedule—for example, as transportation to work three times a week, or as a family activity before supper in the evening.

ROWING. Rowing develops upper and lower body strength, important to cross country but neglected in most running and hiking. Rowing with arms moving in unison works well, but rowing with an alternating stroke is more specific to cross country. Kayaking employs the alternating motion as well. Unlike rowing, however, kayaking (and canoeing) do not exercise the lower body and legs appreciably, and so should be combined with other activities for complete cross country training.

ROLLER SKIING. Roller skiing is by far the most specific of preseason workouts. Roller skis are now widely available in many models, and although they can be expensive (average price is about $150.00), they are worth the investment for the serious skier. They consist of two, three, or four hard-rubber or plastic wheels mounted on a ski shaft. The wheels have a one-way forward motion, so they give traction when you kick backward. Using poles (a bit longer than your ski poles) and standard boots and bindings, you can mimic the motion of skiing on dry land.

Roller ski on the flat or uphills. Some roller skis have brakes and some do not, but in either case downhills can be dangerous. It is also difficult to turn on roller skis, so pick a practice area that is straight and level. Develop your roller-ski skills slowly and safely, as obvious variables make this a more dangerous pursuit than skiing itself. Use roller skis in areas with little traffic. Some parts of the country have restricted or even outlawed roller skiing on public roads, so check with local authorities before you go.

STRETCHING

Stretching before a ski outing is one of the best warmup and prevention routines available. A 10-minute session will loosen your muscles sufficiently to avoid stiffness on the trail when you start out. What follows are nine stretches designed to limber up the most important cross country muscles. Use a thin foam pad for the floor exercises—a camp pad works very well—or stretch on a low-pile rug. Breathe deeply from your stomach as you stretch, and avoid stretching too hard—just to the point where the muscles in question feel taut. You may repeat the exercises as many times as you wish, until you feel loose and stretched.

NECK AND
UPPER-BACK
STRETCH

Neck And Upper-Back Stretch
Lie flat on your spine, knees comfortably bent, feet flat on the

floor. Clasp your hands behind your head and pull up, stretching your neck so your chin touches your chest. Hold for 20 seconds. Repeat several times.

QUADRICEP STRETCH

Quadricep Stretch
Sit on the floor, leaning back comfortably on your hands, legs outstretched. Draw one leg in so that the sole of that foot rests against the opposite knee. Bend your other leg around and back (you may pull gently with your hand if necessary) until the foot lies sole-up on the floor, pointing backward. Hold for 20 seconds. Repeat with the other leg. The farther you lean back, the more the quadricep will stretch.

Plow With Leg Lift Stretch
Lie flat on your back, straight, arms at your sides. Slowly lift your legs to a vertical position, using your hands and forearms for support. Your toes should be aligned over your shoulders or head. Hold the vertical position for 10 seconds, with your arms supporting the weight of your trunk. Then gradually continue the arc with your legs, bending them over your head until they

PLOW WITH
LEG LIFT STRETCH

rest on the floor in a full plow. Hold there briefly, then (using your arms to take the weight) lift your legs in reverse and settle them on the floor, pausing at the top of the arc. Don't crash your legs down; let your arms take most of the weight.

CALF STRETCH

Calf Stretch

Stand upright, facing a wall about one foot away. Cross your arms against the wall and lean your head against them. Draw one leg back, resting the foot flat against the floor. As you do this, the knee of your other leg will bend so that your body leans against the wall from heel to head. Hold for 20 to 40 seconds, then repeat with the other leg. Do not bounce when you are stretched.

Back Roll

Sit on the floor and grasp your bent knees, with your head tucked between them. Slowly roll backward, keeping this position, until your head is on the floor and your feet point upward. Roll several times, stretching your lower back as much as you comfortably can. You may wish to remain in the feet-up position for a few seconds. When done with the final roll, release your knees and slowly roll out flat, resting each vertebra on the floor until your feet touch down.

BACK ROLL

Spine Twist

Sit on the floor and cross your legs, back straight, chin up, arms

SPINE TWIST

at your sides. Put one arm behind you, resting against your spine and horizontal. Turn slowly in the direction of that arm until you can grasp your knee with the opposite hand. At the same time, turn your neck in the same direction, until you look over your shoulder. Hold for 20 seconds, then repeat with the opposite arm.

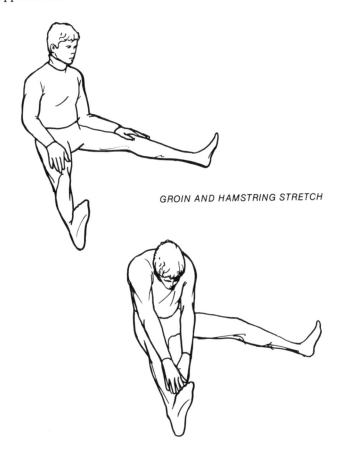

GROIN AND HAMSTRING STRETCH

Groin And Hamstring Stretch
Sit comfortably on the floor, legs straight and spread apart.

Touch your foot with both hands at once, moving slowly and with your back slightly bent. Repeat on the opposite side. This one's a real stretcher, so don't hold the position longer than is comfortable (usually about five to 10 seconds). If you can't reach your foot, rest your hands on your shin at first, and gradually move forward as your muscles loosen up.

SIDE AND ARM STRETCH

Side And Arm Stretch
Stand upright, arms at your sides, legs about two feet apart. Rest one hand on your hip and raise the other arm straight above your shoulder. Without twisting, bend sideways so the raised arm arcs over your head toward the floor. Bend at the waist as you stretch. Hold for 20 seconds, then repeat on the opposite side.

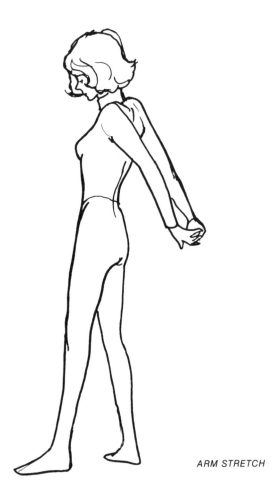

ARM STRETCH

Arm Stretch

Stand erect, arms at your sides. Clasp your hands behind your back and raise them as far as you comfortably can. If you twist your wrists so that your interlocked forefingers move apart, you will stretch your inner forearms and biceps. This stretch also does wonders for your spine.

The above exercises are best performed at home, just before you ski. Sometimes, though, you may be an hour's drive or more from your skiing spot or touring center. If that's the case, here's a set of quick stretches you can do standing, without an exercise pad.

First, run through the standing calf stretch, side and arm stretch, and arm stretch described above. Then try the spine twist, standing, with your right arm behind you and your left hand grasping your right shoulder. Repeat on the opposite side.

Standing, stretch your arms straight above your head, then bring them down slowly in the classic touch-toes exercise. Repeat four to seven times, stretching slowly and deliberately. Don't bounce if you can't reach your toes at first; just hold the full stretch a bit longer each time.

Finally, stand with your legs spread apart. With your spine straight, sink slowly on one side, bending that knee and keeping the other leg straight, until the thigh muscles of that leg are fully stretched. Hold the position for 20 seconds or so, then slowly rise to standing. Repeat on the other side, then repeat both sides four to nine times.

CHAPTER FOUR

SKI SCHOOL

T he old saw has it that cross country skiing is just like walking. Experienced skiers know this is true and untrue at the same time. It is like walking because you so frequently employ the same basic mode of locomotion—the diagonal stride, with alternating arms and legs going forward and back. It is not like walking because you are adding a dimension that doesn't exist on dry ground: the glide. So what you are really doing is interpreting walking in a manner that will propel you across the snow. Sound simple? Well, truth be known, it is.

However, as with any discipline, cross country skiing can be refined to a sophisticated level involving numerous techniques. This chapter is not intended to be a full instructional reference on how to cross country ski. It is a look at the fundamental techniques upon which the advanced skills of the sport are built. The 12 techniques and maneuvers described here are the basic skills you need to handle the level ground, uphills, and downhills you will encounter during most day tours and while skiing at touring centers.

Let us recommend two excellent books to study for a full course in technique: John Caldwell's best seller, *The Cross Country Ski Book*, and Michael Brady's *The Complete Ski Cross-Country*. Along with—and more important than—written instruction we recommend personal instruction from qualified teachers. The best guarantee of receiving good instruction is to seek teachers that are certified by the Professional Ski Instructors of America (PSIA). Most touring centers maintain a teaching staff that is PSIA certified.

DOUBLE POLE
One of the first things beginners learn is to double pole, propel-

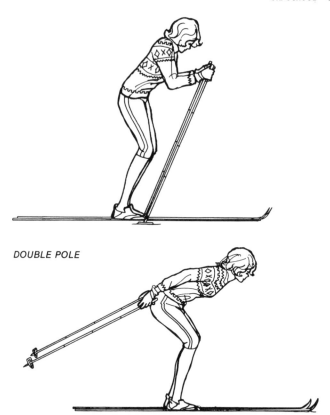

DOUBLE POLE

ling themselves ahead, skis together. Take both poles forward and plant them at a comfortable reach, push down and back, and release the poles behind with a smooth follow through. This is an excellent way to accustom yourself to the feeling of skiing and getting about on the snow. But after a while—say, after going 50 yards or so—you'll notice a certain drawback to the double-pole technique. It's hard work! You'll see clearly that to travel on the level or slightly uphill, there have to be better ways. There are, and they are discussed below. After you've reaped the double pole's benefit as an early way to accustom yourself to the feeling of this new sport, you'll save the technique for extra speed on the downhills and flats.

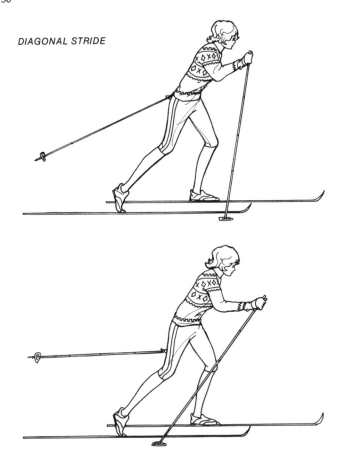

DIAGONAL STRIDE

DIAGONAL STRIDE

The fundamental technique in cross country is the diagonal stride. Here, instead of simply walking about, as you take a step you push off with one other foot (or ski) to propel yourself forward onto your other foot (or ski). Then you glide on that foot as you prepare to repeat the process with your gliding foot becoming the new kicking foot. One foot kicks, the other steps forward to glide, then the other foot kicks while its counterpart steps forward to glide.

The better you are at cross country skiing, the more glide you will get for each kick. A truly proficient skier will make a decisive kick and then move ahead in a long, smooth glide. The expert's body stretches out with each stride. If you watch this skier closely, you'll see something else that characterizes his movement: His motion is concentrated straight down the track or trail; there is very little up-and-down or side-to-side, wasted motion.

What to do with your arms and ski poles during the diagonal stride? As in walking, you are striding diagonally: The right arm goes forward to plant the pole as your left foot is stepping forward, and vice versa. Follow through smoothly, then swing your arm and pole forward for the next pole plant.

To handle uphill grades with the diagonal stride it is necessary to shorten your movements. This is because your glide is shortened. You can maintain the diagonal-stride rhythm, but your pole plants will not be as far ahead of you and your kick will not extend as far back. Compared to the fully extended diagonal stride on the level or slight grade, striding up challenging hills resembles jogging on skis. The steeper the grade, the more you have to shorten your reach on the pole plants and your strides themselves.

38

SKATE

SKATE
This technique is not beyond the intermediate or the fast-learning beginner. This—you guessed it—is just like skating. Imagine the rhythmic flow of a skater in Rockefeller Center.

Don't think of the kids plunging forward in the pick-up hockey game, knocking over all who get in the way. Think of the guy, hands clasped behind his back and scarf flung casually about his neck, who pushes deliberately off one skate onto the other and glides ahead smoothly to the easy tempo of a Viennese waltz. Well, skating on cross country skis is very much the same thing. You push off with the inside edge of one ski and step forward to glide with the other ski. You haven't got your hands clasped behind your back like the ice skater, but you do have them at your side. Double poling accompanies the skate, but you should reach only about half as far forward as you would when double poling without the skate. The poling motion should coincide with the push off each ski. You'll have to be a little more deliberate in your push off and step forward than the ice skater—that's because your cross country skis are much longer than the skates' blades. But the overall rhythm and movements are quite similar.

The skate is useful when you are on a trail that has no set track or under any conditions when your wax or waxless base won't give you enough grip; in the skate you gain purchase with the inside edge of the kicking ski, not with the base of the ski.

You can skate with an alternating motion—right ski to left ski to right ski again—or you can take a series of pushes off one ski before switching, which many cross country racers do.

FALLING DOWN

Everyone falls once in a while (at least). Falling can be divided into two categories: premeditated and unpremeditated. You can't do much about the unpremeditated falls except to cut their number by using common sense and maintaining an awareness of your skill level. Perhaps that downhill is a bit too challenging and you should sidestep down carefully—or even take your skis off and walk down. Fools rush in where angels fear to tread.

In the event you are confronted with a downhill that you aren't sure you can handle but want to try anyway, look for an escape route should you lose control. This is important when skiing trails that wind through the woods. Those thick-trunked trees can come at you at an alarming pace. Think about whether there will be people behind you to warn or if there are people in front of you who are likely to fall and you are likely to run over if you don't give them time to get out of the way.

If you misjudge a downhill and find yourself losing control, it may be time to bail out—certainly you should if the grade steepens or a sharp turn is approaching. The classic bail-out maneuver is simply to sit down on the snow. Keep your skis facing forward, knees and ankles together, hands to your sides with ski poles pointing back. Then grit your teeth, swallow your pride, and sit.

You will find countless variations on the classic sit maneuver, many of which will certainly be spur-of-the-moment inventions that cannot be duplicated, but the concept behind the basic technique of falling should be observed if possible: Make your progress to the ground as careful, and painless, as you can.

Now this may sound a bit silly, but, yes, we recommend that you practice falling. Many people fall because they are tense and afraid of falling. But if they knew beforehand that anyone can do it and that it's usually harmless, they might relax and avoid falling altogether.

GETTING UP

Getting up after a fall can pose a problem at times. You may have to roll onto your back and swing your skis around in the air to place them downhill of you. Then stand up, with the aid of your ski poles if necessary. If you use your poles, don't place them between your skis; plant them in the snow uphill of your skis. Place your skis downhill of you and across the fall line—or face—of the hill. If you try to get up with your skis uphill you'll probably fall again. If you get up with your skis pointing downhill—you're off and running again. If all else fails, of course, you can take your skis off, stand up, and put them back on again.

Whenever skiing on groomed trails, try to avoid damage to the tracks when getting up and repair the damage you may have caused.

TUCK

TUCK

When you encounter a downhill on the trail that doesn't require stopping or turning (or falling) the basic technique for riding it out is to assume the tuck position. In the tuck position you are reducing wind resistance and lowering your center of gravity by bending at the waist and knees and tucking your ski poles, pointing back, under your arms. You can rest your forearms on your thighs. With your knees bent and legs relaxed, your legs will act like shock absorbers to handle minor irregularities in the trail. If you want to go faster, you can raise up, reach forward with your poles, and double pole, keeping your skis together.

SNOWPLOW

A basic technique for slowing down, turning, and stopping is the snowplow. You just create a wedge (ski tips in and tails out) that acts like a snowplow to slow your progress. You can accelerate by reducing the width of the wedge and decelerate by making it wider. In the snowplow you exert pressure to the in-

SNOWPLOW

side edges of the skis. You can vary this according to terrain by using a half-snowplow, where you simply put one ski in the wedge position and keep the other facing straight downhill. The half-snowplow is very handy when descending a trail too narrow for a full snowplow.

You can also use the snowplow to turn. Exerting greater pressure on the inside edge of the right ski will turn you to the left. Exerting greater pressure on the inside edge of the left ski will turn you to the right. After making the turn, you can bring the skis back together in the parallel position or you can continue the snowplow according to terrain.

If you exert equal pressure to the inside edge of both skis in a full snowplow you can bring yourself to a stop.

During each of the snowplow maneuvers described above, you should keep your arms hanging loosely and comfortably at your sides with your ski poles pointing to the rear.

STEP TURN AND SKATE TURN

STEP TURN AND SKATE TURN

To make a step turn, as you approach a turn in the trail you pick up the ski that will lead into the turn and place it back on the snow, facing into the turn. This requires unweighting this ski. After replacing on the snow, you unweight the other ski and pick it up to place it alongside. You may want to take a series of small steps to accomplish a turn.

If you push off the weighted inside edge of your ski when placing the other ski into the turn, you've made a skate turn. The skate turn is quicker and can be sharper than the simple step turn, and it requires a little more practice to master, but it is very handy when faced with making a sharp turn at high speed.

STEM-CHRISTY TURN

STEM-CHRISTY TURN AND STOP

The stem-christy turn is like a half-snowplow turn. You begin by setting the inside edge of one ski against the snow in the wedge position of a half-snowplow. As the turning process begins, you accelerate it by committing your full weight to that inside edge, bringing the other ski parallel to the edged ski. At this point you will have come around in the turn and you can distribute your weight equally on both skis again.

On narrow trails that require quick, decisive turns the stem christy is useful because it allows you to make quicker, sharper turns than does the snowplow or skate turn. On wide, open slopes it is fun to link a series of stem christies together as you come down the hill.

Unlike the snowplow, in the stem christy you will want to keep your arms about chest high, bent at the elbows. When you begin the turn you can plant the pole on the side you are turning to and use it as a pivot—not so much to anchor your turn, however, as to provide balance for committing weight to the downhill ski.

You can also stem christy to a parallel stop. This is a faster, more decisive stop to be used on steeper grades than the snowplow stop. As with the stem-christy turn, you begin by weighting the inside edge of the downhill ski. After you commit your weight to that ski, bring the uphill ski parallel and weight the outside edge of that ski. This will bring you to a stop the same way that an ice skater sets his skate blades against the ice to stop in a parallel position.

HERRINGBONE

When a hill is too steep to conquer with your diagonal stride, you can herringbone up it. Spread your ski tips out and bring the ski tails in to form a wedge. By weighting the inside edge of one ski you gain enough purchase to step forward, up the hill, with the other. You should adjust the width of the wedge according to the steepness of the hill—tails closer together, tips farther apart the steeper the grade. In some uphill situations, a half-herringbone is all you need; just place one ski in the wedge position and keep the other pointing straight up the trail.

There is no glide in the herringbone. You are actually climbing the hill, step by step. However, it is possible to maintain a

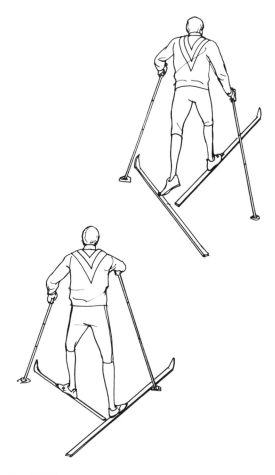

HERRINGBONE

diagonal-stride rhythm as you climb.

With each step, plant your ski pole behind the foot of the edged ski in a comfortable position to help the ski give you the necessary grip to step forward with the other ski.

SIDESTEP

SIDESTEP

The sidestep is used on hills that are too steep for either the diagonal stride or the herringbone. It is laborious on long hills, but on very short, steep rises it is a quick and effective way to get up and over. In this maneuver you stand sideways to the slope of the hill. Begin with weight on the uphill edges of both skis, then unweight the uphill ski, take a step up, plant it, bring the downhill ski up alongside it, and repeat. Always keep your weight on the uphill edge of each ski.

Generally, when you step up and plant the uphill ski, you also plant the uphill pole and use it to help gain grip to bring up the downhill ski. The downhill pole is planted downhill of the downhill ski and brought up when the ski is brought up. In some very tough situations, however, especially in off-track touring, you may want to plant both poles downhill of the downhill ski to give the purchase and balance needed to take the uphill step.

KICK TURN
The kick turn is a simple technique for making a 180-degree change of direction in a stationary position on level terrain, and it is also very useful during steep switchbacking climbs. With both skis parallel, you pick up one of them, swing it to the outside around your pole, and place it facing the other direction (or as close to the other direction as your muscles allow). Then you bring the other ski around to the parallel position again. Simple

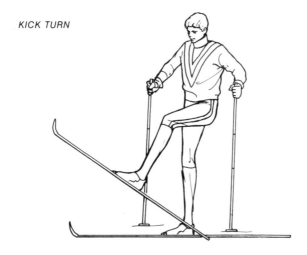

KICK TURN

as that, you are facing the other direction. However, your cross country skis are long, tangly creatures, and you'll have to remember to raise your feet up high enough to clear the tips and tails when swinging them around.

During the kick turn your poles are planted out to the sides in

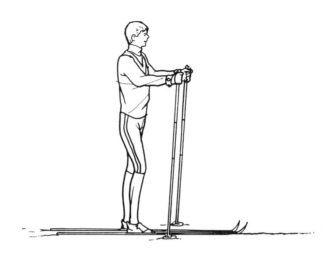

a comfortable position to help maintain balance, and then moved and replanted as the skis come around and your position changes.

Mastering these 12 techniques will open the door to skiing proficiency for you—and they will also lead you to more specialized techniques, particularly if you discover a love for downhill skiing on cross country skis. Such advanced techniques as the telemark turn, full parallel downhill skiing, and others are described in the two books mentioned at the beginning of this chapter and in books about cross country downhill skiing specifically, such as Steve Barnett's excellent book *Cross Country Downhill*.

CHAPTER FIVE

WAXING

Many beginning skiers worry about waxing. They think it's a mystery, or worse, a hassle. It isn't. When all is said and done, waxing is nothing more than a straightforward, effective way of assuring proper grip and glide under all snow conditions. It can be as simple as the two-wax system or as complicated as a racer's secret "klister cocktail." At all points, though, waxing follows a set of rules you can learn in a relatively short time. And as you learn these rules, you'll also learn about types of snow, winter weather conditions, and how your equipment relates to your technique. Follow the guidelines below, practice them when you ski, and you'll soon discover what lifelong skiers already know: Waxing's not only pretty easy, it can be downright fun.

THEORY

To work well, wax must do two jobs. First, it must provide enough friction between ski and snow for the skier's kick to move him forward with each stride (skiers call this friction grip or purchase). Second, the wax must allow the skier to glide over the snow during the glide phase. For wax to do both may seem like a contradiction, but it really isn't. It is more of a balancing act between properties of different waxes and properties of the snow.

This is how wax provides grip: A fresh snowfall consists of innumerable snowflakes in the familiar six-sided pattern. When a skier stands on his skis the sharp edges of these snow crystals dig into the wax a fraction of an inch, giving him something to push against as he kicks backward. The deeper the crystals penetrate the wax, the more grip the skier has on the snow.

This is how wax allows glide: When the gliding ski is in motion, friction between the wax on the running surface and the snow creates a thin film of water under the base of the ski. The ski glides on this film rather than on the sharp snow crystals.

If the snow crystals dig too deeply into the wax during the kick, they'll stick and hinder proper glide. Likewise, if the crystals don't dig deeply enough into the wax, the skier won't generate enough friction to move forward. A balance between the sharpness of the crystals and the hardness of the wax is the goal.

TYPES OF WAX

There are three basic types of waxes for cross country skiing: kick wax that provides grip, glide wax that enhances glide, and binder wax that improves the ski base's retention of kick wax. The glide and binder waxes should be applied in your home or workshop before skiing, and their application is easy. Kick wax, however, is usually applied just prior to skiing and frequently reapplied or changed while on the trail. This is because kick wax must correspond to snow conditions on different ski tours or even to changing snow during a single tour.

The proper application and choice of kick wax is critical to skiing enjoyment, and this is where the correct balance between wax consistency and snow conditions must be found to provide both grip and glide. Let's consider kick waxes first, and then go on to the simpler techniques of glide- and binder-wax choice and application.

TYPES OF SNOW, TYPES OF KICK WAX

From the moment it reaches the ground, snow undergoes a series of changes. The sharp edges of new crystals soften, become duller, and eventually disappear as sun, wind, and temperature affect them. Water content—the amount of free, unfrozen water in the snowpack—changes as the snow melts and refreezes. The changes that snow undergoes can generally be described as moving from sharp crystals to rounded crystals.

Just how many types of snow there are is the subject of much debate. Snow metamorphoses along a continuum upon which any number of discrete points may be found. For our purposes, though, let's consider the three basic types of snow: powder snow, wet snow, and klister snow.

POWDER SNOW. New-fallen cold snow is called powder. It has sharp edges, is light and fluffy, won't pack into a snowball, and is dry (all the water in the snow is frozen). Powder is the coldest snow, and usually occurs when temperatures are well below freezing. After a while, powder snow "sets up" into packed powder. Warmer temperatures may increase its water content, but it generally remains dry and grainy to the touch.

WET SNOW. This occurs when snow falls at or near the freezing point or when powder snow warms up. It feels wet, packs easily into a snowball, and is heavier than powder snow. Its crystals are rounded and dull. If wet snow is on the ground when days are sunny and nights are cold, it can form a crust on top, ranging from a thin layer of ice to the infamous "boilerplate."

KLISTER SNOW. Klister snow is snow that has melted and refrozen. Certain types are also called frozen granular, corn snow, or blue ice. This snow has no sharp edges and is usually wet. Often it looks and feels like tiny beads of ice. When the sun warms klister snow, it can quickly turn to loose, wet granular or even icy mush.

Since there are different kinds of snow there are different kinds of kick waxes. A hard wax that works fine with powder snow won't allow klister snow to penetrate far enough to provide sufficient grip; conversely, a soft wax ideal for old, rounded crystals will grip too much in powder. This leads to the first rule of choosing a kick wax: The warmer (or wetter) the snow, the softer the wax; the colder (or drier) the snow, the harder the wax.

Wax to provide grip comes in two basic types, hard waxes and soft waxes. The soft waxes are also called klisters. For powder snow and wet snow, hard waxes are used. These are sold in cannisters or cakes, and have the same consistency as a crayon. Klister waxes have a gel-like consistency; they usually come in tubes and are extremely sticky. Klisters are used for snow that has melted and refrozen (metamorphosed).

Given these broad categories, how do you choose the right wax? The solution is air temperature, because air temperature affects the nature of the snow crystals. Wax companies, having spent years in research and development, have adopted systems of color coding based on outside air temperature; each wax col-

Klister waxes, because they have a soft, gel-like consistency, come in tubes for ease of application. Hard waxes come in tins. Shown in the foreground are a plastic wax scraper and two klister applicators. The klister applicators are used to smooth out the sticky soft wax after it has been dabbed onto the ski base. At right is a synthetic cork used to smooth hard waxes.

or corresponds to a different hardness of wax. As a rule, you can choose the wax you'll use based on these temperatures. For example, say the temperature is about 25 degrees Fahrenheit and the snow is fairly fresh; checking a chart (or the information printed on the side of the wax can), you find that blue hard wax has a temperature range of 23 to 31 degrees Fahrenheit. In that range, blue wax will give you the proper balance of grip and glide, and your choice of wax should be blue.

As an extra guide, many wax companies choose "cold" colors for their harder waxes, and "warm" colors for their softer waxes. Thus, Swix waxes, for example, range from green through blue, purple, red, and yellow as air temperature increases. (But remember that two waxes of the same color made by different companies may not match precisely in temperature range. It's a good idea to familiarize yourself with a particular brand, one commonly available in your area, and stick with it.)

APPLYING HARD WAX. Back in the days of all-wood skis, skiers usually waxed the entire length of the ski, from tip to tail. This worked well enough, but advances in equipment and wax technology have made it unnecessary. Today, most skiers apply kick wax only to the wax pocket—the area in the center of the ski base that presses against the snow when you kick. It is here that kick wax is effective. If it is applied too far in front or behind the wax pocket, on the running surfaces of the ski, kick wax tends to slow you down.

Precisely how long your wax job should be—how much of the wax pocket you should cover—is learned by experience. Some skiers with a strong kick may want only a short length of wax; others will want it longer. In general, the beginning waxer should wax from about one and one-half to two feet in front of the toeplate to just under the heelplate of his binding.

First, make sure the base of the ski is clean and dry. Wax indoors if it's convenient, with the ski at room temperature (this will help wax retention, or the ability of the wax to stay on the ski longer).

Starting at the top of the wax pocket—ahead of the binding—crayon the wax onto the ski base in long, smooth strokes, as far back as the heelplate of the binding. You don't have to rub hard, just enough so that a thin layer of the wax adheres to the base. Cover the entire width of the ski on either side of the central groove. Try not to get wax into the groove; the groove is there to provide proper tracking, and wax will diminish its effectiveness.

To apply hard kick wax, peel back the wax tin to expose the wax, and crayon onto the wax pocket of the ski base.

After the hard wax is crayoned on, smooth it out with even strokes of the waxing cork. Try to keep wax out of the ski's central groove.

The next step after you have rubbed a thin layer of wax onto the ski base is corking it in. Corking wax into a base smooths out the wax layer and aids in wax retention. Starting again from the top of the wax pocket, rub the cork down the wax layer in smooth, even strokes. The key here is smoothness, not strength. If you stroke evenly, with moderate pressure, you will generate enough heat between the cork and the wax to warm and soften it, thus smoothing it sufficiently.

After you have applied a layer of wax and corked it in, repeat the process. Rub another layer of wax over the first layer, then cork it in, always moving from the front to the rear of the wax pocket. Several thin layers of wax, as opposed to one thick layer, are desirable for both smoothness and wax retention. Applying two or three layers may seem a bit like overkill at first, but the difference is dramatic; you are far less likely to have to stop and rewax on the trail.

That's it. Now you're ready to ski. If you have chosen the right wax and applied it correctly, your kick will be effective and your glide long and smooth. The feeling of perfect balance between kick and glide—skiers call it "hitting the wax"—is like nothing else in the world; once you've felt it, you won't forget it.

Of course, you may not hit the wax right off. Sometimes conditions change, sometimes you don't choose the correct wax. If your wax job doesn't feel quite right, think TLC—Thicker, Longer, Change. First, make the wax layer *thicker*; apply another thin layer or two of the same kick wax and cork in well. If you still aren't getting proper grip, try *longer*; extend your wax job farther toward the tip and tail of the ski. Finally, *change*; use another wax, either colder or warmer, according to conditions.

Another rule to keep in mind when waxing for grip is to avoid putting a layer of colder wax over a warmer wax. The warmer wax is softer, and if you layer a harder wax over it, the harder wax will rub off into the snow in no time. It's fine to put a layer of warmer wax over a colder one, but if you have to change from warm to cold (soft to hard), remove the layer of warmer wax first.

APPLYING KLISTER. Klister is the bogeyman of waxing. Most new skiers have heard nothing but horror stories about it, and almost no one loves handling it. Klister sticks tenaciously to everything it touches—fingers, clothing, fanny packs, car doors, everything. But if you apply it correctly, you won't make a mess of things. And it's the only wax that works on snow that has melted and refrozen—spring snow, corn snow, warm weather and sunny day snow. Skiing in those conditions is an awful lot of fun, and skiing with klister can be the best skiing of

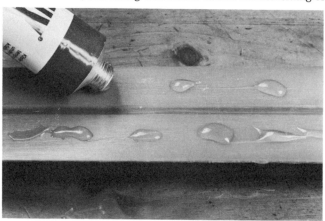

Applying klister wax for kick doesn't have to be a messy chore. Dab on the wax in the wax-pocket area as shown.

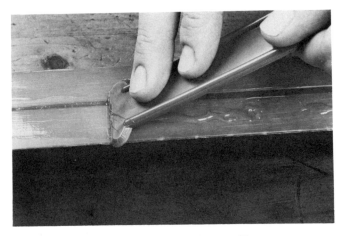

Spread the klister evenly with the wax applicator. (Most wax companies supply an applicator with each tube of klister.) If necessary, be sure to clean central groove of the base with the rounded edge of the applicator to insure proper tracking of the ski.

the year.

Because it is semisolid, klister comes in tubes, like toothpaste. Klister is color coded according to temperature: blue, purple, silver, red, and yellow. Silver is the most versatile of these; it is often mixed with other klisters to improve wax retention, and it sticks like mad when used properly.

To apply klister, first make sure that the ski base is clean and dry. It helps to have a torch, waxing iron, or similar heat source nearby, because warm klister spreads more evenly and easily than cold, thick klister. You can warm the tube of klister with a few quick passes through the flame of the torch. Starting from the front of the wax pocket, squeeze a thin squiggle of wax on either side of the central groove, all the way to just under the heelplate of your binding. Or you can daub the klister onto the ski in evenly placed spots. Don't squeeze the tube so hard that you have klister running all over the place. Just use enough pressure to apply it in a thin layer.

Many wax manufacturers include a plastic spreader with each tube of klister. Using the flat end of the spreader, make long, smooth strokes over the klister, until the klister is spread evenly over the entire width of the ski on either side of the groove.

Spread from front to back, as always, drawing the klister flat with the edge of the spreader. Once it is smooth and even, that's that. No corking is needed.

It's always a good idea—with hard waxes as well as klisters—to set your skis outside for a few minutes after application. This cools the wax and improves retention. If you need to switch klisters because you've guessed wrong or conditions change, remember what was said above about hard wax: a softer klister over a harder one is okay, but not the reverse. Remove the first layer and start over again with the right wax.

THE TWO-WAX SYSTEM. Waxing for grip can be as simple or as complicated as you want to make it. In our discussion of kick waxes you've seen that wax is color coded by most companies according to temperature. There are many variations within this, and several specialized waxes within a given color—blue, blue extra, blue special, and so on. For the novice skier, all these different waxes may seem a bit daunting. For them, and for some experts who like to keep things simple, a few companies have come up with a simplified approach—the two-wax system.

The two-wax system divides snow into two types, wet and dry. Wet snow is warmer snow, the kind you can easily mold into a snowball. Dry snow is cold snow; it is powdery or grainy

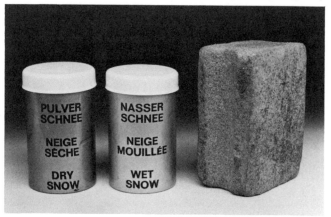

With the two-wax system all you need is one wax for wet snow and one for dry. These are applied and corked in like any hard wax.

and won't form a snowball. For each of these, the system provides one wax, each of which is a hard wax. Applied like hard wax, it takes the place of all those greens, blues, reds, and other waxes. It's that simple.

But if the two-wax system works so well, how come it hasn't replaced the traditional kick waxes? In a word, the answer is performance. The wet and dry waxes of the two-wax system work well enough, and they are an excellent introduction to the principles of waxing. But they are general. Traditional kick waxes are far more specific to temperature and conditions—and within those conditions, they work better than anything else.

REMOVING WAX. After each outing, the kick wax should be cleaned from your skis. This will not only make storing your skis easier and less messy, but it will also assure that your skis are clean and dry the next time you want to wax. There are three ways of removing wax: with a scraper, with a torch, and with wax remover. Hard wax can be removed with any of these. Klister should be removed with a torch or wax remover.

Scrapers are made of plastic or metal. For the novice, a plastic scraper is preferable, because it's less likely to gouge the base. To use a scraper, grasp the ski or clamp it base upward on a waxing bench. Scrape straight down the ski, using the edge of

Wax remover acts as a solvent to the wax. Apply to a rag or piece of fiberlene and wipe the ski base. Wax remover is both flammable and poisonous, so be sure to read cautions.

Removing wax with a torch is easy and efficient. Simply heat the wax to a liquid state on the base and wipe off with a rag or a piece of fiberlene. Be careful not to overheat the ski base, which will ruin it, and be careful to let your right hand know what your left is doing when handling the torch.

the scraper flat against the base. As wax collects on the scraper, wipe it off and repeat the process until all wax has been removed from the base. Check the edges of the skis and the central groove to make sure no wax residue remains (most scrapers have a rounded corner to dig wax from the groove; if yours doesn't, swipe a spoon from the utensil drawer at home .

Wax remover is a solvent that liquefies wax so that it can be easily removed. To use, soak a bit into an old rag or a piece of fiberlene (a special rag material available from wax companies, ideal for this purpose), and wipe the wax off the ski. It may take a few passes, so be sure that all wax has been removed before you quit. Because wax remover tends to dry out many base materials when used frequently, clean any leftover remover from the base after use. Some experts also recommend rewaxing the ski with a protective base wax after cleaning it with chemical remover. Wax remover is both poisonous and highly flammable, so keep it out of reach of children and read the cautions on the can before using.

To get a ski really clean without wax remover, many skiers use a propane torch. A torch is highly effective, but requires a good deal of care to use. The principle is simple: Holding the torch, you make a few quick passes with the flame over a small portion of the wax, heating it to a liquid state. Rub the liquefied wax off the ski base with a rag or fiberlene. Remember, though, to let your right hand know what your left hand is doing; keep the flame well away from the base as you remove the liquefied

THE ESSENTIAL ON-TRAIL WAX KIT

Your "essential wax kit" contains everything you'll need on the trail on a given day, and nothing more. Experience will teach you to amend this list as you wish.

WAXES. Take along the first wax of the day, the one that outside temperature indicates is the correct wax. Also, take a wax or two at either end of the expected conditions—say, green and purple if the wax of the day is blue. The wider the range of conditions you expect to confront, however, the more waxes you'll want to take along.

If the day calls for klister wax, remember to take along a spreader. For ease of application, keep klisters close to your body; that way they'll stay warm and soft. Always be sure that the tube of klister is closed tightly before returning it to your pack, or you'll have a nasty mess on your hands at the end of the day.

SCRAPER. This should be carried along in case you have to remove a hard wax on the trail.

CORK. You'll need a cork to buff wax in when the time has come to rewax. Unless you insist on traditional materials, get a synthetic cork; these generate more friction than natural cork, warming the wax and making application easier.

THERMOMETER. Winter weather can be tricky. The temperature can get warmer or colder in a hurry, so it's a good idea to carry a thermometer along to consult before changing waxes. It will give you a reliable indication of changes in the weather and show you how weather alters waxing needs. Try one of those tough little plastic ones on a key chain, and hook it to your jacket zipper or outer layer of clothing. If you keep it too close to your body, you won't get an accurate reading of air temperature.

WAX CHART. Most wax companies provide wax charts as an accessory. You can use this in conjunction with your thermometer to choose an alternative wax if the one you started with isn't working. This book includes wax, or you'll scorch your fingers. And watch out where you point the torch when you're concentrating on wiping wax off.

BINDER AND GLIDE WAXES
In addition to kick waxes, two other types of waxes are used for

a wax chart on the back cover.

TOWEL. This, which can be a square of an old terrycloth bath towel, an old bandanna, or some folded-up paper towels, will aid in drying the ski base if you have to make an on-trail wax change.

WAX REMOVER. In the event you must take a layer of wax off your skis in order to change to a colder wax, you can bring along a small container of wax remover. You will probably have to improvise on the container, selecting a vessel that is of convenient size, closes securely, is non-soluble, and is unbreakable. You can use the towel mentioned above to wipe remover off, but if you're using klister it is best to take along a separate klister rag for this purpose.

Your essential wax kit fits easily into a fanny pack or a compartment of your day pack. It holds what you will need for a day's outing: scraper, cork, thermometer, wax of the day (plus a couple extra for insurance), a wax chart, and a bandanna or cloth to clean and dry the ski base before applying wax.

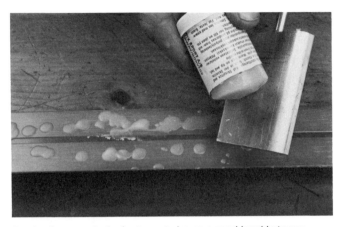

Heating in waxes is the best way to insure a good bond between wax and base. It is handy for applying glide and binder waxes, but is also recommended when convenient for applying hard and soft kick waxes. Begin by heating the waxing iron and holding the wax against it to dribble melted wax onto the base.

cross country skiing. The first of these, glide wax, improves glide. The second, binder wax, improves wax retention. Both types of wax, while not absolutely necessary, enhance your skis' performance. Both are well worth the extra time it takes to apply them.

Glide waxes are very hard waxes applied to the tips and tails of your ski. You may rub them on and cork in like hard kick waxes, but because you want these waxes to adhere well to the ski base, it is best to apply them indoors, using a torch or waxing iron. The heat from either of these does two things: First, it warms the wax so it can be applied smoothly and thinly; second, it causes the small pores within the ski base to expand and accept the wax more readily (this is often called—erroneously—wax "absorption"). A torch is sufficient, but an iron, either a special waxing iron or an old clothes iron, does the best job.

If you choose an old clothes iron for waxing, set it to the medium or medium-high setting. If you use a waxing iron, simply heat it with the propane torch. Some wax irons have electric heating elements.

To apply glide waxes with heat, first check to see that your ski base is dry and free of all other waxes. Set the ski base in a vise

Reheating the waxing iron with the torch as needed, iron the wax
into the base.

or on a waxing bench, horizontal and firmly in place. You'll
want both hands free for the job ahead.

Once the iron is heated, hold it over the ski base at an angle
and place your cake of wax against it. The wax will quickly melt
and start to dribble onto the base. You don't need to cover the
whole base with dripping wax. Just melt enough for a couple of
thin lines on either side of the central groove, from the tip of the

Scrape excess wax until you are left with a smooth, thin layer.

Be sure to take the rounded edge of the scraper to clean the central groove of the base. If your scraper doesn't have such a corner, a spoon makes a good substitute.

ski to the top of the wax pocket and from the bottom of the wax pocket to the tail. That done, rub the iron over the wax in smooth, even strokes. Because this warms the base as you stroke, the wax will be "absorbed" and will stay longer on the base. After rubbing, set the heating iron aside and let the wax cool. Then scrape the wax down until it is very thin, and buff it with a cork. Scrape any excess wax from the sidewalls and central groove of the ski.

Glide waxes should be applied as needed, though not as frequently as kick waxes. A good rule of thumb is to check the tips and tails after each outing. If the base looks whitish, it means the wax has worn off and it's time to apply another layer.

You might have guessed by this time that a torch or waxing iron may also be used to apply hard kick waxes and klisters. Absolutely. Heating in is the best way to apply any wax. The practice for kick waxes is the same as described above for glide waxes. But use a torch for klisters, because they can make an awful mess of a waxing iron; pass the flame lightly over the klister until it is completely liquid. With a little experience, you'll find that heating in waxes doesn't take much time, works like a charm, and helps mightily in wax retention.

Binder wax is used as an aid in wax retention. It helps hold kick waxes to the base in old, abrasive snow, and icy, hard-

CARDINAL RULES OF WAXING

Throughout this chapter, certain guidelines about waxing with kick waxes have appeared. These are rules to remember whenever you wax. Though waxing is an inexact science, what follows holds true for almost all waxing situations.

CLEAN AND DRY. Before applying any waxes make sure the ski base is clean and dry.

WARM OVER COLD. You can layer a warmer wax over a colder wax, but not the reverse. If you layer a colder (harder) wax over a warmer (softer) wax, the wax will quickly rub off into the snow, and you'll have to start all over. Save yourself the hassle and remove the softer wax before applying the harder wax.

TIP TO TAIL. Always apply wax in one direction, from the front of the ski to the back. When corking wax in, stroke from tip to tail as well.

SMOOTH AND EVEN. A smooth, even layer of wax along the entire width of the ski will give you optimum kick and glide. Clumps of wax, ridges, furrows, and other irregularities collect dirt and cause excess friction.

LAYER YOUR WAX. Several thin layers of wax will last longer and give you better performance than one thick layer.

TLC. When your wax isn't working, adjust the wax job in this order: thicker (another layer of wax), longer (extend the wax farther along the wax pocket), change (go to a different wax, colder or warmer depending upon conditions).

packed tracks. Binder need be applied infrequently, when conditions are harsher than normal. As a tacky, sticky hard wax, it should be applied with a waxing iron, indoors, on a room-temperature base, and only in the wax pocket (you may use paraffin wax as a binder in the glide zones). Melt the binder over the base of the ski in the manner described above, then scrape it down and buff it with a cork. Let the wax cool completely before rubbing kick wax over it. Don't melt kick wax into a base prepared with binder; this may mix the sticky binder with the kick wax, resulting in skis that drag.

CHAPTER SIX

PLANNING AN OUTING

W hat could be more pleasant than a day tour on cross country skis? It's the ideal winter escape—a sure cure for cabin fever and a chance to stretch office-weary limbs. At the minimum, all you need is a day pack, your ski gear, some good friends, and a place to go. You won't set any altitude records on a day tour or earn the *coureur de bois* distance medal, but when you're finished you can go home refreshed to a warm fire, a hot drink, a big dinner, and a fluffy bed. In this chapter we'll look at how to plan a day tour to make sure you have a good time: where to go, what to take along, and some hints on how to enjoy the day to the fullest.

WHERE TO GO

Day touring means skiing close to your base, whether your base is a condo in Brooklyn or a lodge in the northern Cascades. The route can start from your back door or from a trailhead a couple of hours' drive away. It can go through city parks or along a riverbank—anywhere there's snow and access is permitted. To figure out where to go, the first thing to determine is how far to go. This depends on the skill level of the group. Experienced skiers hitting the trail right after breakfast may want to ski as far as 30 or 40 kilometers or more before nightfall. Beginners, especially those unused to spending long periods in the cold, will want to ski shorter distances—10 kilometers or less. It's impor-tant for a group to pick a route and distance that everyone will be comfortable with, or the day won't be much fun. And remember the skill level of your group is only as high as that of its *least* skilled member. There will be plenty of time for longer tours when beginners have gained the skill to enjoy them.

In planning a route, think ahead. What's available? What is

the general lay of the land? Are there interesting sights along the way? Can you make a wide loop to return or should you double back? And where's a good place to stop for lunch? You don't need to overplan, but knowing where you're going keeps the route within the bounds of reason. An unexpected winter bivouac may be thrilling to some, but it is an emergency situation with possibly dire consequences.

In The City And Suburbs
City parks, riverfronts, along the beach after a fresh snow, anywhere the city opens up to let a little snow in can provide the route for a day tour. Try to avoid motorways if possible; respect for skiers on interstates is minimal at best. Many cities in North America are developing skiing programs in their parks and other public places, among them Toronto, Minneapolis, and Chicago. Cities generally have only limited facilities for skiers, but use your imagination and check with appropriate sports shops and parks commissions to find out what's available.

In the suburbs, golf courses are excellent for day touring. The terrain is varied, open, easy enough for the beginner, and big enough to satisfy exercise fanatics. You'll make the owners happy if you ask permission first—you may even find that they have a regular winter skiing program (stay off the tees and greens; golfers are sensitive about them). Parks are great, too, of course, and you can find out where the high school's cross country running or skiing team practices. Nature centers throughout the country are starting winter programs as well, and there you can combine skiing with nature-study tours.

Ski Touring Centers
Touring centers are perfect for day tourers. With very little preparation, you can be out on the snow all day long. It's a different sort of experience from bushwhacking, more organized and civilized, but consider the advantages: Most centers groom and track their trails, offer maps, and provide such services as waxing rooms, rental equipment, ski lessons, and even cafes and snack bars. Besides, you get to meet all sorts of other cross country enthusiasts. If you haven't been to a touring center, by all means go.

One very big advantage of ski-touring centers results from a groomed and track-set trail. For beginners, a well-maintained trail is much easier to learn on, because obstacles such as deep powder or heavy wet snow are removed, and the tracks themselves are easier to ski down as they provide guidance and stability to your skis. For more advanced skiers, the groomed terrain allows them to concentrate on developing technique. For racers, a well-maintained track is required to practice on, because it simulates the conditions of most race courses.

At a touring center, too, you need not carry the full day's gear with you at all times. Beyond a simple wax kit, a few items of extra clothing, and perhaps a candy bar and some water, you can leave the gear that might be needed later in the day in the car. You can even leave all behind but your skis and the clothes on your back for a quick spin of two or three kilometers near the warming hut or lodge. You'll be back before the weather changes drastically or you require food or water.

In The Country

In the country you can ski almost everywhere—all you need is snow. You can chase along miles of farmland, follow a favorite summer hiking path, wander by a river, or ski wood and meadow to a country inn. Wherever you go, ski touring in the country is the essential cross country experience.

A day tour in the country is a fairly simple proposition. There are, however, some basic rules you should always keep in mind and special situations to think about before you leave.

If you plan to be skiing away from others for a full day, have at least three people in your group. In case of injury, one can go for help and another can stay with the injured person. Before you leave on such a tour, also make sure someone knows where you are going and when you plan to return.

Winter weather can change rapidly, often without warning. Know what the weather's supposed to be like all day long, and plan for contingencies. Will it be windy? Take along extra clothing and skin protection. How cold will it be at higher elevations, or inland if you live near the coast? Will it snow? You'll get wetter and colder if it does, so shorten your route accordingly. And remember, if you're driving home, that snowy roads are slippery and will slow your return.

If you ski in the woods, keep to paths or areas where you

won't lose your sense of direction. If you ski a hiking path, make sure it's wide enough to accommodate turns and bail outs, especially on the downhills. If you think you may head off your planned route, give yourself time to double back and follow your tracks to the trailhead.

If you are touring through unfamiliar territory, you should always carry a map. Maps come in all shapes and sizes, but usually the best and most complete are topographical maps produced by the United States government. These are available through ski shops, outdoor shops, parks headquarters, and through offices of the United States Geological Survey.

Topographical maps illustrate natural and man-made features such as roads, water sources, trails, place names, elevations, and political boundaries. They are produced on a north-south, east-west longitude and latitude grid (with north at the top of the map) and include scales and other information necessary for accurate interpretation. Used with a compass, a topo map can tell you exactly where you are and how to reach your destination.

The science of map and compass is called orienteering. It requires study and practice to understand thoroughly, and we won't attempt a complete explanation here. There is, however, a simple method of direction-finding you can employ when you are on the trail.

At the trailhead, open the map and find the declination scale. This is a wedge of two lines at the bottom of the map, just to the left of the mileage scale. The line pointing directly to the top of the map shows the true north; the line at a slight angle from true north shows the magnetic north (that is, the direction to which the compass points). Set your compass over the declination scale and turn the map until the north point of the compass is aligned directly over the line of magnetic north. The true north of the scale is now pointing straight north, and your map is *oriented* to the terrain, with all the vertical lines aligned in a true north-south direction.

Now that your map is oriented, you can pick out features on the map that correspond to the terrain. Look at the area on the map surrounding your trailhead and note streams, hills, and other features along your proposed route of travel. If, for example, the map indicates a hill a mile due west from your

Orienteering—finding your way with map and compass—is a science unto itself. However, a simplified method of direction finding will help you plan a safe day tour within your skiing abilities.

present location, look for that hill in that direction. Reading elevations on a topo map requires a bit of practice—they are shown as brown lines of regular "contour intervals" that run closer together as steepness increases and farther apart as the land levels out. The lines are marked by elevation, though, and a few minutes of study will show you which hill has the same general shape and elevation as the one in question.

When planning a route with a topo map—or any map—be especially conscious of streams. In periods of runoff in the spring or after a thaw in the winter even small streams can become raging, uncrossable torrents.

As your tour progresses, consult the map frequently, checking natural features and your direction of travel down the trail. Try to avoid areas where the contour lines of the map run closely together; this indicates steepness, and may prove to be tough going on skis. Keep in mind, too, your position relative to roads and other routes back to civilization. If you know, for example, that a road runs a mile west of your route, in an emergency you can find it by traveling due west.

By all means, don't tour by map and compass until you have first had practice in areas you know well. Orienteering, as mentioned above, is a science, and requires thorough study to be of use to you.

The best introduction to orienteering we've found is a book called *Orienteering For Sport And Pleasure* by Hans Bengtsson and George Atkinson. Further information, including training sessions in your area, is available from the United States Orienteering Federation, P.O. Box 1039, Baldwin, Missouri 63011. Maps from the United States Geological Survey may be obtained locally or by writing the Branch of Distribution, United States Geological Survey, Federal Center, Denver, Colorado 80225 (for maps west of the Mississippi River) or the Branch of Distribution, United States Geological Survey, 1200 Eads Street, Arlington, Virginia 22202 (for maps east of the Mississippi).

Despite their lack of appeal for some, snowmobile tracks make easier going through the woods than unbroken powder. If you come upon one, though, be careful to keep an ear out for traffic—it's a safe bet they'll not hear you first. Other routes that tend to be easier are wide hiking paths along rivers (less elevation change), and evergreen stands with little undergrowth. Snow conditions in large fields can be tricky—stick to the woods' edge for easier going and conditions similar to those in the woods.

One big advantage to the country is the wide degree of acceptance cross country skiing enjoys among private landowners. In addition, there are many parks and wildlife areas maintained by state and federal agencies that welcome skiers. Remember, though, that you are a guest of the private owner and a patron of the public park. Obtain permission to ski if you need it, and register at the park office if you're supposed to. Cross country's good reputation depends on courtesy and responsibility from all skiers.

WHAT TO TAKE ALONG

What to take along on a day tour depends upon where you're going. If you're off for a day in the woods, below is what you should take. If you are going for a half-day's ski in the country or if you plan to visit a touring center that has some facilities you can adjust this gear accordingly.

WAX AND REPAIR KIT. This can be stored in your day pack or a group member can carry a fanny pack with everything for the group's waxing and repair needs. Bring along your "Essential Wax Kit," which is described in Chapter Five. These

CROSS COUNTRY COURTESIES

Though you may frequently plan a day tour with the thought in mind of finding some solitude with companions, many times you will encounter other skiers on the trail—and especially if you are touring at a developed ski-touring center. Below are "Rules of Conduct for Cross Country Skiers" developed by the International Ski Federation to make skiing simple and safe.

A cross country skier must ski in such a manner that he does not endanger others.

A skier should always adapt his speed to his personal ability, to the prevailing visibility and terrain, and to the traffic on the course.

Keep to your right upon meeting an oncoming skier. A climbing skier should give way to a descending skier.

A skier should ski in the right-hand track when there is more than one track set.

Trail-marking signs must be respected. On any trail marked with an indicated direction, a skier should proceed only in that direction.

A skier is permitted to overtake and pass another skier to the left or right. The skier ahead is not obligated to give way to the overtaking skier but should allow a faster skier to pass when he judges it possible.

Keep poles close to the body whenever near another skier.

A skier who stops should leave the tracks. In case of a fall he should clear the track without delay.

When an accident occurs, everyone should render assistance if necessary.

Witnesses to an accident should establish their identity.

Add to this list common sense and a healthy respect for private property (with regard to litter as well as trespass), and you should be able to handle any on-trail questions of etiquette or right-of-way you encounter.

items should answer all your waxing needs for the day. In addition to the wax kit, the following repair items should be brought along as well.

Spare ski tip. This is available at most ski shops. It's a plastic tip that slips over the front of a broken ski. It may be rarely used, but is a real lifesaver when the need arises.

Duct tape or fiber tape. Strong tape can be used to lash broken poles, tape a boot back together, even to fashion a makeshift binding when all else fails. You will find many uses for this item.

Screwdriver. This must fit binding screws. Check to see that it's the right kind before you leave. Some pocketknives have a screwdriver blade that can be used to tighten binding screws—but because it's a fold-out blade it is sometimes difficult to use as a screwdriver due to its tendency to fold in when rotated under pressure.

Spare binding parts. These may be extra bails for 75-millimeter bindings or extra parts if you have another system.

Pocketknife. The pocketknife is an old pal of outdoorspeople, and it has innumerable uses. The Swiss Army style knives have many features—from awl through corkscrew—that come in handy.

Spare pole basket. Skiing without a pole basket, should one break, is no fun. It is difficult and tiring, especially in unpacked snow. Bring along an extra one just in case.

Boot laces. Spare boot laces are welcome should you break a lace on the trail.

WATER. Cold weather is deceptive. You don't always feel as thirsty as you would in the summer. Cross country skiers lose lots of water through perspiration and breathing, and the last thing you need on a day tour is a sudden case of overheating from dehydration. You should sip water (or tea, coffee, hot cider, cocoa) often, even if you don't feel thirsty. If it's a half-day tour, carry at least a quart for each person, and more to be on the safe side. Don't worry about the weight; you'll drink it up soon enough.

Alcohol is not recommended as liquid replenishment while ski touring. Because alcohol dilates the capillaries of the skin, more body heat is lost when alcohol is consumed. This can contribute to chilling, loss of energy, and eventually, hypothermia. This does not mean that the springtime corn-snow-and-chablis picnic lunch is taboo, it means use common sense and depend on water and other drinks to replace spent liquids.

FOOD. Food is a big part of a successful day tour. A tasty lunch is something to look forward to all morning and an energy boost for the afternoon. Although what you bring is mostly a matter of preference, high-energy, easily prepared foods have a distinct advantage over heavy, high-bulk foods. The body can metabolize high-energy foods—carbohydrates and simple sugars—faster than it can other foods. When you're out on the snow, you don't want to sit around for two hours after lunch digesting, so carbos and sugars are in order.

Some foods are so classic for day tours as to be almost *de rigeur*: fresh or dried fruit, cheese, bread, and crackers are all favored, along with some sweet treats like chocolate (be careful not to overdo chocolate; it's loaded with fat and can cause stomach cramps when you're exercising). Nuts and seeds are great, of course, along with cut-up vegetables, smoked meats, and peanut butter with jam. Soup from a Thermos is warming and welcome and saves you the trouble of bringing along a weighty stove if you want something hot. Try what you like: Your menu is limited only by your imagination and willingness to make lunch a special stop.

Food shouldn't have to wait for lunch, though. In fact, it is a better idea to snack throughout the day and eat a light lunch, for this creates an even production of energy without requiring your body to perform digestive gymnastics as well as ski maneuvers. Along the trail you can munch away at any of the above or other convenient rapid-energy foods, such as gorp. Stuff a granola bar or two into a pocket, keep an orange handy, or take some hard candy along. You use up plenty of energy on a day tour; small, frequent feedings keep your energy level high and revive the spirits if you begin to tire.

EMERGENCY AND FIRST-AID KIT. Unfortunately, accidents will sometimes happen. An emergency and first-aid kit doesn't have to be large or fancy, just enough to cover the bases. In a group, one person should be responsible for this kit and know how to use it. For a list of what goes into this, see Chapter Seven.

GORDO'S GORP

And what would a ski tour be without gorp? It's the journeybread of modern times. Here, for the first time, we reveal our own secret, high-energy, never-fail gorp recipe.

1 cup chocolate bits (or carob if desired)
1 cup chopped almonds
1 cup cashews
1 cup salted peanuts (or unsalted spanish peanuts)
1 cup sunflower seeds
1 cup chopped, dried apricots
2 cups raisins (or currants)
½ cup chopped dried apples
¼ cup flaked coconut, if desired
2 cups oats
3 tablespoons oil
¼ cup maple syrup or honey

In a large bowl, blend oats, oil, and maple syrup. Spread on a cookie sheet and bake in an oven at 275 degrees, turning occasionally. When oats are crisp (about 45 minutes), remove, and cool. Mix with remaining ingredients. This recipe makes enough gorp for 16 skiers, and it may be reduced proportionately.

EXTRA CLOTHING. This is especially important. Wet socks or gloves can be very uncomfortable and even dangerous when frostbite becomes a possibility. Follow the layering system and bring along a spare windbreaker, spare socks, gloves, and a cap (wool caps can become soaked with sweat and freeze your ears in no time). Be careful around frozen ponds and open water—no sense in getting an unnecessary dunking—and bring spare clothing along, just in case you do. Chapter Two gives information on clothing to help you make the right choice of spare items.

MISCELLANEOUS. You may take along toilet tissue, sunglasses, any necessary medications, skin protection (if you're skiing in higher altitudes or during the spring—get a glycerin-based or lanolin-based sunscreen or protective gel to protect exposed flesh from sunlight and wind chill), a timepiece, and of course, a map and compass. If you will be skiing near civilization, take along some money for snacks, carfare, or pay telephones. Bespectacled skiers should bring some antifog treatment (available at most drug stores) for their lenses.

SKIING WITH CHILDREN

Children require attention on a ski tour. If you ski with children, make sure the route is easy enough and short enough so they won't become exhausted. Bring along plenty of spare clothing for them and take frequent rest stops. Also, ski slowly enough so that the children don't feel they're holding up everyone else.

Children aren't aware of cold-weather precautions, so it's up to adults to check frequently for signs of frostbite or hypothermia. At the first sign of chilling—shivering or teeth chattering—stop, warm the child's ears or hands with your own hands, and maybe change his hat or other clothing. If you are skiing with very small children—backpack-carrier size—dress them warmly. They won't be exercising and need extra protection from winter's cold. Check their faces and hands frequently and keep the tour short. An insulated sack/sleeping bag helps to keep a child warm. And don't forget the baby food or the diapers (and a plastic bag in which to store the used ones!).

Children need to feel they are partners in the tour. A small backpack, with snacks, toys, and some clothing, makes them feel they are carrying their own weight. Each child should also have an adult "buddy" to look after him and see that he is having a good time. The buddy can make up games, point out trees and wildlife, and give the child a real adventure.

SKIING WITH DOGS

A lot of controversy exists over whether or not to take the dog on a day tour. Of course, the dog loves it, and it's great to be out in the woods with your best friend. Trouble is, dogs don't know the safety rules of skiing. They can rush into the way on downhills and cause a nasty spill. Their pawprints and leavings can ruin tracks for skiers who follow you and they can build up painful iceballs between the pads of their feet in icy conditions. If you're out in the woods, dogs may disturb and even kill wildlife, many forms of which are especially vulnerable in winter. Regrettably, there are just too many problems skiing with dogs. If you're going to ski where any other skiers will ski, it's best if Fido stays at home.

CHAPTER SEVEN

SAFE SKIING

O n a moonlit night two years ago, a friend of ours went cross country skiing on a golf course. Coming down a gentle rise at moderate speed, he fell, landing on his upper leg. At first he thought he had only bruised himself. But when he tried to move he realized his injury was serious—bad enough, in fact, that he knew he should not try to move again.

He was with three companions. It was in February, and the temperature was 10 below zero. Fortunately, there was no wind. One friend, the strongest skier, skied to the nearest phone—just a quarter-mile away. There he called the local rescue squad. The other two friends laid on the ground with the injured skier to keep him warm. When the rescue squad finally arrived two hours later, the injured skier was transported to the ambulance and rushed to the hospital.

Our friend had broken his femur, the upper thigh bone that is the strongest in the body. "People who break that bone," said the surgeon, "have usually been hit by a truck."

Subsequent testing showed that he had no previously undetected bone diseases and had simply taken a spill on a gentle, golf-course downhill. Ironically, earlier that afternoon the same party of four had skied up *and down* the highest mountain in the region on steep, switchbacking, ungroomed hiking trails at breakneck speed.

All in all, however, our friend was lucky. He escaped hypothermia and frostbite and in time his leg healed. Last winter, he was off to Yellowstone Park to ski the backcountry. But *if* there had been a severe wind chill factor, *if* the already tardy rescue squad had been tardier, *if* his companions had panicked, the story might have ended quite differently.

The lesson here is to be wary of lulling statements that proclaim how safe cross country skiing is compared to alpine skiing and other winter sports. "Safe" and "safer" are relative conditions. By learning basic cold-weather precautions and emergency techniques, you can make your skiing as safe as possible. And the confidence that creates will help you relax and enjoy the sport as it should be enjoyed.

Treatment of physical trauma such as sprains, fractures, and concussions should be learned under the guidance of a qualified first-aid teacher. Anyone who spends a good deal of time outdoors—winter or summer—should look into local first-aid courses offered by the Red Cross, the YMCA, ski clubs, hospitals, and rescue squads. In this book, we will discuss basic precautions you should take before your tour and describe procedures for emergencies that might occur on a one-day tour. Bear in mind that we're only scratching the surface here. For full education about winter camping or ski-mountaineering emergencies, you should seek qualified instruction such as that provided by The Outward Bound School, the National Outdoor Leadership School, or local organizations.

In the previous chapter on planning an outing, we covered things you should do before you take off on your tour. Here, for special emphasis on safety, we want to repeat precautions that should be standard procedure before you leave.

INFORM SOMEONE OF YOUR PLANS. Let someone know where you will ski, the route you will follow, and when you plan to return. If you do not return on time, he can notify authorities and request that a search be initiated. If you change your plans after the tour—you decide to stop for drinks or dinner, say—let him know at once so your tardy return won't cause him to sound the alarm and send search parties stomping off into the mountains needlessly.

CHECK WEATHER CONDITIONS AND TIME OF NIGHTFALL. Weather predictions have a direct bearing on your choice of supplemental clothing and route. Always plan for contingencies. Don't plan a trip that will challenge you to get back before dark.

CHOOSE A SENSIBLE GROUP SIZE. If you are off on an all-day tour that will take you beyond shouting distance of civilization, three members is the minimum group size. If someone is hurt, one can stay with the injured skier while the other

---

YOUR PRETRIP CHECKLIST

In this chapter we have talked about precautions to take before you head out on a day tour. These are listed below in summary form. If you have chosen a route and assembled the necessary gear as described in the previous chapter, these additional safety-oriented precautions will round out your preparations.

Inform someone of your plans.
Check the weather forecast and time of nightfall.
Choose a group size to complement the tour.
Choose a tour leader.
Doublecheck your gear.
When in doubt, don't.

Following these simple guidelines will help you avoid contingencies that might not only spoil the day but also end the day tragically.

---

skis for help. Figuring maximum size is more difficult. But when your party grows toward 10 or more, things tend to become a bit unwieldly.

CHOOSE A LEADER. Mountaineering expeditions always do, and for a very good reason. The buck has to stop somewhere when critical decisions must be made. Your day tour certainly won't be a mountaineering expedition, but it could involve situations when quick, clear, decisive action is essential. A leader is invaluable for dealing with these contingencies. The function of a day-tour leader is to assess quickly all factors in an emergency, solicit opinions, determine options, and then choose the best course of action. This person should be designated at the outset by the group, with the understanding that his judgment in crisis will be followed. He should be the strongest skier, the most experienced backcountry traveler, and, perhaps above all else, the most level-headed. Your particular party may not include a single individual who possesses all of these qualities, but generally in any group one individual will stand out as the person to trust in adverse situations.

CHECK YOUR GEAR. Look over all the gear you'll be taking along on your tour. Pay particular attention to the following to make sure age or damage will not lead to on-trail equipment failure: ski pole straps, baskets, and shafts; bindings (screws, bails, and other moving parts); boot laces and upper-to-sole attachments; ski tips for fractures and delamination. Check the contents of your repair kit and your first-aid kit. Check your map and compass and flashlight and batteries.

WHEN IN DOUBT, DON'T. If you are in doubt about anything when planning, from choosing a route to deciding whether the car has enough gas to get back from the trailhead—play it safe. Always err on the side of caution. Remember Murphy's Law.

If you follow the above guidelines, you will avoid many problems on the trail—and you will be prepared for accidents and emergencies that may happen. Following is a list of the more common emergency situations and—briefly—ways to keep them from becoming catastrophes.

CAUGHT AFTER DARK OR IN A WHITEOUT

Even the best-laid plans can go awry. If you are caught by darkness or by whiteout (dense fog or blowing snow that makes travel just as difficult as darkness), you have two options: You can continue, or you can bivouac. Being caught short of your destination by darkness or whiteout can be unsettling, and requires forethought before choosing an option.

Decide to keep moving only if you know your course and terrain well enough to ski it in low or zero visibility. You will need to distinguish landmarks by faint moonlight or starlight or, in the case of a whiteout, to navigate by compass alone. If you're traveling on a trail that leads directly back to your starting point, your difficulties are substantially reduced. But if you're bushwhacking, skiing above timberline, or using a trail system with multiple forks, your situation is more complicated. Keep in mind the possibilities for wrong turns that may confront you during your return leg and weigh them objectively against the value of pushing on in limited visibility. If it is easier to walk out than ski out, take off your skis and hoof it. Above all, be sure before going ahead.

If you decide to push on, maintain constant contact between all members of your party, and pay attention to the weakest member's physical and mental condition. You don't want to reach your trailhead to find someone is missing.

In some situations, a bivouac is the sensible alternative. If you decide to bivouac, several immediate tasks confront you. Shelter is your first priority. You should also take an inventory of food and water and decide how to ration your available supplies. And you must plan what to do in the morning when the light of day will tell you where you are.

The best shelter is one that provides maximum protection for the least amount of work. If you can find a cave, a circle of

---

AN EMERGENCY KIT FOR SKIERS

Ready-made first-aid kits for the kitchen or automobile may not be all you need for taking along on the ski trail. You will find a greater need for some items and little for others. You can assemble a simple first-aid kit that best suits the day tourer and at the same time add items to expand the kit into an emergency kit as well.

ANTISEPTIC. This is for sterilizing cuts and lacerations. Try to find a product that resists freezing, such as antiseptic powder.

GAUZE AND ADHESIVE TAPE. Gauze pads and half-inch-wide adhesive tape may be used to form bandages of varying sizes.

ACE BANDAGE. Wide elastic bandages, such as the Ace bandages, may be used if a trick knee requires it or for other functions, such as a makeshift sling. It is also handy strapping for an emergency splint.

KNIFE. This can be like your pocketknife, with many attachments, but is primarily a back-up knife with a reliable cutting edge should the pocketknife be lost.

COMPASS. You will be using one map and compass during tours to unfamiliar territory, but a second back-up compass, like the knife, takes up little space and is a special measure of insurance.

MATCHES OR LIGHTER AND CANDLE. Place strike-anywhere matches in a waterproof container; if they can't be struck anywhere, enclose a striking surface, too. Disposable butane lighters are also good as an emergency fire source, but since it is hard to tell how much fuel is left, you should take two along. When such a lighter is cold the gas is reluctant to escape, and the lighter may require warming with your hand to work effectively. Test the lighters before heading out. A brand-new lighter should snow protected by thick evergreens, or even a thicket created by a deadfall, you can usually improvise adequate protection from wind and blowing snow with minimal effort. Failing these assists from nature and if snowpack is sufficient, you can build a simple snow trench or burrow into a snowbank. In either instance, use your ski tip as a shovel to dig or carve out blocks of snow. Having dug a snow trench, roof it with ski poles, skis, poncho, branches, or any other material that will prevent heat

also be tested. A candle is invaluable for fire-starting in wet conditions.

FLASHLIGHT. A portable flashlight will help when you must travel in darkness. Check batteries before each outing. Many companies now supply simple, inexpensive headlamps (such as those worn by miners) that keep both hands free for skiing.

SURVIVAL CARDS. These are plastic cards with all manner of survival information on them, and they take up less space than a wallet. A fine set of these cards is available from Survival Cards, Box 1805, Bloomington, Indiana 47402.

WHISTLE. A whistle will help a search party find you if you become lost. At timely intervals you can signal SOS (three short blasts followed by three long blasts followed by three short blasts).

DUCT TAPE OR FIBER TAPE. This has a thousand and one uses. Carry a full roll.

If your day tours take you into country where avalanche hazards exist, add the following to your list of emergency items.

AVALANCHE BEACON. This item is useless without knowledge of its function. Drill *all* party members in its use before setting out.

SHOVEL. A collapsible shovel is essential for travel in avalanche country. Its function is straightforward in avalanche conditions. It is also valuable if you are forced to bivouac, for it can be used to help build a snow shelter.

PROBES. Convertible ski poles are the best, and several models available commercially are designed especially for avalanche search-and-rescue operations.

from escaping. Snow is an excellent insulator and may be thrown or packed over these materials. Protection from wind is essential.

If you work hard enough to perspire during your shelter building, change clothes or change the order of your layers to put dry clothing next to your skin.

If you are certain to find your way out the next day, use your remaining food and water as you wish, keeping enough aside for tomorrow's travel. If you are likely to be out for another night, ration sensibly. A person can last several days easily without food, but water is more critical. If you do not have a backpacking stove to melt snow, you will have to find natural water sources—streams or melting ice, for example. If there's any chance of hypothermia, it's best not to melt snow directly in your mouth—taking it that way can further reduce your body's core temperature.

In your bivouac shelter, put on all your extra clothing, and stick your feet into your pack. Share body heat with companions if the cold is severe. Jokes, stories, and songs can help keep spirits up. Your bivouac, if you must make one, is not an unforeseen danger. It is an eventuality for which you have planned and for which you are prepared.

GETTING LOST

If you plan your tour carefully this contingency will not arise. But it can occur on even the best planned tours if violent weather conditions arise or another situation in which gear—your map and compass—is lost as well as your sense of direction. Being found by a search party, however, depends heavily upon having informed someone of your plans, as recommended above.

If you are lost, first follow your tracks back toward your destination as far as the tracks allow. Do not, however, follow any tracks if you suspect they are circuitous, which is probably the case if you are lost. Also, wind-blown or falling snow may obscure any tracks.

Once you've backtracked as far as you can, your priority becomes staying put. Create a marker of some sort. This may be a fire, to which, once you have it burning well, you add wet branches to make a smoke signal. If you are nearby an open field, choose an article of clothing and stake it out with branches, skis, or ski poles. Choose an article of clothing that will contrast with the snow. However, since most searches are organized as ground, not air, searches, a smoke signal is recommended. But both are best.

Once the marker is created, prepare to bivouac following the instructions given directly above under "Caught After Dark Or In A Whiteout." Follow the directions for food rationing and staying warm also given in that section. Remember that you can last longer without food than without water, so give priority to melting snow or locating a water source nearby. Avoid melting snow in your mouth to obtain water. Also think about available clothing and gear and how best to use these items.

At timely intervals, if your whistle has not been lost, give an SOS signal (three short blasts followed by three long blasts followed by three short blasts). Or whistle with your fingers if you know how. This will help the chances of being located by a ground search.

Precious heat-creating calories will only be lost if you panic. A simple one-day ski tour should not take you so far from civilization that you will not be found in a matter of time. Stay put, stay warm, stay in touch with the physical and mental conditions of party members, and stay calm.

GETTING WET
If you fall into a stream, if the ice breaks on a pond, or if you get soaked for any reason, get out of the wet clothes and into dry garments as soon as possible—even if you don't feel particularly cold. If the temperature is a balmy 40 degrees Fahrenheit, it is still 58 degrees below your body temperature—and you will lose heat at an alarming rate if you are wet and exposed to a gentle wind. If extra clothing is lacking, different members of your party may be able to contribute items to form a makeshift outfit.

FROSTBITE
Frostbite occurs when body tissue freezes. It almost always afflicts the extremities—fingers, toes, exposed portions of the face—and is most likely to occur in severely windy conditions. There are several early warning signs of frostbite, and all

members of a party should monitor themselves and other party members for these signs.

Numbness is the first and most noticeable sign. It means that blood circulation to the affected area has ceased. If circulation is not restored, the flesh will freeze and frostbite will occur. Whitening of skin tissue, often called "frostnip," is another early warning sign. In very cold, windy weather, exposed portions of the face are likely to suffer frostnip, and sharp-eyed skiers can warn their fellows of frostnip's onset.

Frostnipped or frostbitten tissue should *not* be rubbed with anything—snow, a mitten, even another person's hand. Frozen skin is very vulnerable, and vigorous rubbing can damage it further. The best method for treating superficial frostbite is simply to place a warming surface against the frozen area. The warming surface can be a hand, a foot, a cheek —anything that will transfer heat from the unfrozen tissue to the frozen. If a body part is used, switch fairly often, as heat will drain from it and the ability to warm will be reduced. When color and feeling return to the frozen skin, be sure to surround it with extra insulation; frostbitten skin or flesh is more likely to suffer from cold than previously unaffected tissue.

If the frostbitten area does not respond to skin-to-skin warming after 10 minutes, a *little* more heat is called for. If you've brought along a backpacking stove, fire it up and heat water to a point slightly above skin temperature—about 110 degrees Fahrenheit (use your waxing thermometer to measure water temperature). Either immerse the affected area in the warm water or soak a cloth and apply it to the area.

Deep, solidly frostbitten tissue requires different treatment. Do not thaw the affected area. Leave the hand, foot, or other body part frozen and evacuate the injured skier immediately. Frozen tissue is more likely to be damaged if it is thawed and used than if it is kept frozen until professional medical treatment is available.

Children must be checked frequently for frostbite, because they are less likely than adults to recognize symptoms.

Stay alert to dropping temperatures and rising winds, and do not hesitate to abort a trip if worsening weather makes frostbite probable. When tempted to continue a trip in the teeth of a howling gale, with temperatures dropping, remember the cardinal rule: Err on the side of caution.

HYPOTHERMIA

Hypothermia occurs when your body's core temperature drops to a dangerous level. It is not a hazard reserved for Everest climbers, Alaska expeditions, and the like. It is a danger to anyone who ventures into the woods in cold weather. In fact, the weather need not be very cold for hypothermia to strike; the United States government estimates that most hypothermia cases develop in air temperatures between 30 and 50 degrees Fahrenheit. This is true for several reasons, but the largest factor simply is that people who are outside underestimate the likelihood of hypothermia. Fifty-degree air feels deceptively warm, especially if it is still air. But consider how cold 50-degree water would feel and how quickly your body would lose heat in water at that temperature. Remember, as well, that when you are outside the air around you is rarely still. Even if there is no measurable wind, when you move, you create your own wind-chill factor.

If the foregoing makes you want to forget about skiing altogether, it shouldn't. You can easily avoid this danger with advance planning. Further, early hypothermia symptoms are unmistakable, with remedies that are simple and failsafe. You just need to understand the phenomenon and prepare yourself to combat hypothermia at the earliest stages.

Hypothermia is a lowering of the body's core temperature. You can withstand a certain lowering of this temperature, but beyond that point, your physical and mental functions become impaired. And once your ability to move and think is impaired, chances are you're only going to get worse.

Obviously, the best treatment for hypothermia is prevention. Before you set out on your day tour, consider the two greatest hypothermia creators: wind and moisture. Will your route be exposed to high winds much of the time? Can you seek shelter in timber or below ridgelines? What is the weather forecast? What can local rangers or meteorologists tell you about wind and weather patterns typical of your chosen area at the time of year you're going? And what about moisture? You should be aware of snow or rainfall predictions, of course. Beyond those, consider that an arduous route with many steep climbs will expose

---

MAKING A SLED FROM SKIS

If a hypothermic or otherwise injured person requires evacuation, you can build a simple sled from the injured person's skis for transporting him.

Remove bindings from the skis. Remove the baskets from the ski poles and break the poles in half to create four lengths. Placing these lengths at even intervals, lash them to the tops of the skis with duct tape. Branches and spare clothing laid on top can create a measure of comfort on this sled. Lash ski poles to the sled ski tips to pull it along. The sled may also be used as a stretcher.

---

you to a different kind of moisture: perspiration—which is just as wet as rain or melting snow and can contribute just as easily to hypothermia. Stream, lake, or river crossings over ice or snowbridges present the unpleasant possibility of a dunking. If many of these are contemplated, you might want to truck along a bigger day pack to carry a full change of dry clothing (stored in a waterproof plastic bag in your pack).

Suppose, though, that all your careful planning is for naught. The weatherman's best guess was wrong. The party's tired. You're threatened by wet snowfall, and everybody's been sweating like laborers. How do you check for hypothermia? What to do if you detect it? Following is a consideration of hypothermia symptoms and treatment.

Symptoms

It is paramount that members of a party check on one another for the following symptoms when hypothermia is a danger. As mentioned above, it is difficult to detect these symptoms in yourself and group effort is critical.

UNCONTROLLABLE SHIVERING. Never ignore this. It's an early warning signal that hypothermia has begun, proof positive that your body is fatigued and losing more heat than it can produce. Shivering is involuntary muscle action, the body's emergency mechanism to generate more heat for its chilled core.

SLOW, SLURRED SPEECH. This is another failsafe indicator. It's particularly important to listen for this in other people—and to caution them to listen for it in you—because by the time hypothermia has progressed this far, your thoughts may not be sharp enough to detect the symptom in yourself.

IMPAIRED MOTOR FUNCTIONS. These might include fumbling hands, stumbling gait, abnormally slow walking or skiing pace, and inability to walk or ski without help. At this stage, hypothermia is potentially lethal. Immediate action is called for.

OVERWHELMING DROWSINESS. Lassitude, drowsiness, the irresistible urge to sleep means danger! These are evidence of exhaustion—hypothermia in its terminal stage. At this critical point, instant attention is required to avoid fatal consequences.

Treatment

If you've diagnosed one or more of the symptoms listed above in one or more members of your party, make plans for immediate evacuation of the injured skier or skiers to a hospital or emergency-treatment center. And take the following action.

First, get out of any wind. If you're creating your own wind by moving, stop. Find still air. Get behind a natural wind break, such as boulders, trees, snowbanks, or riverbanks. If necessary, you can set up a wind break of your own with a tent or tarp—or even a screen of bodies if you're in open country and no other shelter is available.

Second, use available clothing to the best advantage. If the victim is wet, strip his soaked garments and get him into dry ones—fast. If he hasn't brought a change of clothing, an assortment of garments taken piecemeal from skiers in better condition can serve as a dry outfit. If nothing else, reverse the order of garments so that a dry layer is next to the skin.

Third, if the injured skier is stable enough to take liquids, feed him warm drinks to raise his body-core temperature. Put him into a sleeping bag, if one is available. If the skier is unable to take drinks, do not attempt to give any. Do not give liquids to a comatose person.

Fourth, if the injured is semiconscious or worse, keep him awake, take off his garments, and put him into a sleeping bag with another person—also stripped. The heat gain from direct bodily contact is appreciable, and may mean the difference between life and death when hypothermia has progressed to this stage.

Any signs of hypothermia should be considered major alarms and sufficient reason for aborting your trip. Beyond simple shivering that is corrected by the addition of a garment or by heat through exercise, plans for evacuation should be made. If the victim is unable to move under his own power, or if it seems that further exertion will make his condition worse, improvise a sled with lashed skis and remove him that way, with other skiers taking turns towing. Again, should a hypothermic person fall into coma, do not give liquids. Insulate the victim with as much extra clothing, sleeping bags, and other items as you can and get him to a hospital without delay. Sophisticated rapid-rewarming techniques have been developed for such cases, but they require trained medical personnel and technical facilities.

AVALANCHES

Avalanche danger remains an underestimated day-touring hazard. We've had the unsettling experience of being caught in a couple of avalanches and have seen many other slides, but most skiers have not. As more skiers explore more winter terrain, however, the contact with avalanche hazard increases. It is very easy for day-touring skiers in many parts of the West, Pacific Northwest, Rocky Mountain States, and western Canada to reach avalanche areas on single-day outings. And avalanches, like frostbite and hypothermia, can strike the day tourer just as easily as skiers on extended expeditions.

The majority of avalanche victims are buried by slides they've triggered themselves. This leads to the obvious conclusion that the best way to avoid this danger is to ski where avalanches don't happen. Easterners and Midwesterners are assured of such safety by virtue of the terrain in their regions. But skiers in big mountain country—those parts of the country listed above—must be selective.

If you choose to travel in avalanche country, carry an electronic avalanche beacon. Avalanche beacons—or "beepers"—won't keep you from getting buried in a slide. Common sense and tons of precaution will do that. But a beeper will greatly enhance your chances of survival should you be caught.

Here's how an avalanche beacon works. Each member of a party wears one on a cord around his neck. The battery-powered beeper, which is the size of a deck of cards, constantly transmits a beeping signal. In the event of burial, surface survivors take out their beepers, switch them to receive, jam an attached earphone into their ears, and begin an immediate grid-pattern search. The closer a receiving beeper comes to one that is transmitting, the louder the received beep becomes. The farther away a receiving beeper goes, the fainter the sound becomes. By moving in a diminishing series of right-angled squares, survivors should be able to locate any burial victim fairly quickly—assuming, of course, that they have a reasonably good idea of where the victim was last seen on the surface. This may not be as easy as it sounds, but a reasonably accurate starting point is one way to diminish search time radically.

It is vital that all members who carry avalanche beacons be thoroughly schooled in their use before having to carry out an actual victim search under high-stress conditions. The best way to do this is to have one person bury a beacon in the snow unseen by the trainees. The trainees are then given a general idea of the buried beeper's location, and allowed a given time period—say, five minutes—to find it and dig it up. If they do not locate it in the allotted time, they should repeat the drill until they are successful.

Beepers are a tremendously valuable aid for avalanche travelers, but they will not keep you from being buried. Do not make the mistake, as some have, of skiing with a beeper in terrain or conditions that you would not ski without one.

Avalanches are complex phenomena, and scientific understanding of their behavior is incomplete. But much knowledge has been gained through research, and we can translate the findings into useful guidelines here. First, you should know that avalanches are affected by two major factors: terrain and weather. Tourers who venture into avalanche country should be aware of the following four terrain considerations.

SLOPE STEEPNESS. Though avalanches occur most often on slopes with a 30- to 45-degree gradient, they can occur on any slope with a gradient of 25 to 60 degrees. If you're contemplating downhill frolics on such slopes, remember the danger zone: 30 to 45 degrees.

SLOPE PROFILE. Slab avalanches, which are the most dangerous, tend to occur on slopes with convex profiles. Slab avalanches can occur anywhere, however, so don't place total faith in a slope just because it appears concave in profile.

SLOPE ASPECT. This refers to the direction the slope faces. In the middle of winter, snow on north-facing slopes is more prone to avalanche. In spring and during periods of sunny days, south-facing slopes are more hazardous. Exposure to wind is also a factor here. Windward slopes (slopes that the wind blows against) usually have less snow, and the snow that is there tends to be compacted, making it stabler. Leeward slopes (those that the wind blows away from) are more dangerous because wind-dropped snow is deeper and deposited in hard formations called wind slabs, which can let go all at once in a major slide. Overhanging cornices also tend to build up over leeward slopes, and the dropping of such a cornice can trigger an unstable slope to avalanche.

GROUND COVER. Naked slopes are more avalanche prone than slopes dotted with brush, trees, and boulders. Again, though, don't be lulled. Even well-covered slopes can and do slide.

There are numerous weather factors that affect avalanche danger, but some of the most important are temperature, snowfall rate, snow-crystal types, storms, and wind. Keep in mind the following cardinal rules.

Very cold temperatures cause snow to remain unstable. When the temperature is near or above freezing, snow settles and stabilizes rapidly. But storms that begin in severe cold and are followed by warmer temperatures are much more likely to cause avalanches.

Rapid weather changes undermine snowpack stability and increase hazard.

Winds of 15 miles per hour or greater that last for any length of time make avalanches more likely, especially on leeward slopes where fresh snow is constantly deposited.

Snow-crystal types can be determined by placing snow against any dark background—parka sleeve, ski surface, sunglasses. Small crystals indicate more avalanche danger than large, star-shaped crystals.

When snow falls faster than one inch per hour, avalanche danger is greatly increased.

Most avalanches occur during or shortly after storms. Be

especially alert to avalanche danger in any area with a foot or more of new snow.

The foregoing information about terrain and weather should be helpful to you, but it is no substitute for a thorough study of avalanches. One of the best books is Edward LaChappelle's *ABC Of Avalanche Safety*. The United States Forest Service puts out an excellent brief publication, the *Avalanche Handbook*, available from the Government Printing Office. There are other excellent sources as well, and you should read as many of them as possible before venturing into avalanche country.

If despite careful route choice and weather observation, you find yourself in avalanche terrain with weather conditions deteriorating to the point where there is a real and present avalanche danger, here is what can you do to keep from being buried. Remember, first of all, that most victims trigger the avalanches that bury them. So keep the following clearly in mind as you travel *out* of avalanche country as quickly as possible.

Avoid skiing over or near visible fault lines—cracks in the snowpack that tend to run horizontally across a slope.

Listen to the snow around you. Hollow, whoomping sounds or cracking noises are indications of high avalanche danger.

Try to keep your travel high by crossing ridges over their tops. Do not ski beneath cornices or across convex slopes.

Look for evidence of past slides, such as cleared swaths of timber or snow runouts, and stay clear of them.

If you must cross a hazardous slope, do so one member of the party at a time. Everyone else should listen and watch the traveler and terrain carefully as he crosses.

Before skiing into such terrain, remove ski pole straps from wrists. Loosen pack shoulder straps, and unfasten hipbelts. Disconnect safety straps and put on warm clothing—hats, mittens, parkas. Disconnecting straps and loosening belts makes it easier to discard ski poles and packs if the slope begins to avalanche, and the extra clothes reduce the risk of freezing in the event you are buried.

If you have to ascend or descend a dangerous slope, ski straight up or straight down. Traversing increases the danger of an avalanche. Use trees, boulder clusters, and other cover whenever possible.

If you are caught in a slide, attempt to do the following.

Discard pack, skis, poles.

Swim to stay on top of the moving snow and work toward the side of the avalanche.

Grab any passing obstruction, such as a tree branch, rocky outcrop, or ice pinnacle, and try to arrest your fall behind the obstacle.

Before stopping, move hands and arms in front of your face, protecting an air space.

Try not to panic. Panicked breathing increases use of your precious air supply.

If you're a survivor, still on top of the snow, take immediate action as follows.

Mark the point where buried members of the party were last sighted and search for them directly downslope from that marking.

Initiate a beeper search—which you should have practiced to perfection before starting on the trip.

Lacking beepers, probe with ski poles, sticks, skis—anything that will penetrate the snow.

Do not leave victims and go for help. After 30 minutes of burial, a victim's survival chances are reduced by half.

Most burial victims die from asphyxiation. Administer mouth-to-mouth resuscitation as soon as possible, and cardiopulmonary resuscitation as well, even if it means leaving a victim's legs and feet buried a few more minutes.

APPENDICES

APPENDIX A
CROSS COUNTRY SERVICES AND ORGANIZATIONS

Below is a list of cross country skiing service organizations in the United States and Canada. Information on skiing destinations, ski-touring centers, and organizations in your area may be obtained by writing these associations. United States Government offices that may likewise be of assistance are listed here.

American Ski Federation, 499 South Capitol Street SW, Suite 406, Washington, DC 20003

Canadian Orienteering Service, 446 McNicoll Avenue, Willowdale, Ontario M2H 2E1

Canadian Ski Association, 333 River Road, Vanier, Ontario, K1N 8H9

National Climatic Center, Federal Building, Asheville, North Carolina 28801

National Ski Touring Operators Association, P.O. Box 557, Brattleboro, Vermont 05301

National Weather Service, Seventh Floor, 5200 Auth Road, Washington, DC 20233

Professional Ski Instructors of America, 3333 Iris, Boulder, Colorado 80301

United States Forest Service, P.O. Box 2417, Washington, DC 20013

United States Geological Survey, Branch of Distribution, Eastern Region, 1200 South Eads Street, Arlington, Virginia 22202

United States Geological Survey, Branch of Distribution, Central Region, Box 25286, Denver Federal Center, Denver, Colorado 80255

United States Orienteering Federation, P.O. Box 1039, Ballwin, Missouri 63011

United States Ski Association, East 1750 Boulder Street, Colorado Springs, Colorado 80909

APPENDIX B
SUPPLIERS OF CROSS COUNTRY EQUIPMENT

Below is a list of manufacturers and distributors of ski equipment and accessories. You can obtain useful information by writing these companies, including product specifications and names and addresses of the retailers near you that carry the specific line of products.

AFRC Ski and Sportswear, P.O. Box 1007, Sioux Falls, South Dakota 57117. *Skiwear*

Action Accessories Incorporated, Buffington Hill Road, Box 271, Worthington, Massachusetts 01098. *Accessories*

Action & Leisure Incorporated, 45 East 30th Street, New York, New York 10016. *Skis, boots, bindings, poles*

Adidas USA Incorporated, 1122 Route 22, Mountainside, New Jersey 07092. *Boots, bindings*

Alpina Sports Corporation, P.O. Box 23, Hanover, New Hampshire 03755. *Boots, bindings*

Alpine Research Incorporated, 765 Indian Peaks Road, Golden, Colorado 80403. *Skis, boots, bindings, poles, accessories*

Alti Products Company Incorporated, 129 West Water Street, Santa Fe, New Mexico 87501. *Skiwear, accessories*

Astrup's Imports, 4516 52nd Street, Kenosha, Wisconsin 53142. *Skis, boots, bindings, poles*

Atomic Ski USA Incorporated, 4 Cote Lane, Bedford, New Hampshire 03102. *Skis, skiwear*

Barrecrafters, P.O. Box 158, Shelburne, Vermont 05482. *Poles, accessories*

Black Ice, 2310 Laurel, Napa, California 94559. *Skiwear*

Colmar, 890 Cowan Road, Burlingame, California 94010. *Skiwear*

Columbia Sportswear Company Incorporated, 6600 North Baltimore, Portland, Oregon 97203. *Skiwear*

Coming Attractions Limited, 1524 Springhall Road, McLean, Virginia 22102. *Skiwear*

Curley-Bates Company, 860 Stanton Road, Burlingame, California 94010. *Accessories*

Denali International Incorporated, Route 1, Box 105, Hidden Wood, Waitsfield, Vermont 05673. *Accessories*

Dermatone Laboratories Incorporated, 1103 Mapleton Avenue, Suffield, Connecticut 06078. *Accessories*

Dovre Ski Binding, 20-60 Beharrel Street, West Concord, Massachusetts 01742. *Skis, boots, bindings, poles, accessories*

Early Winters Limited, 110 Prefontaine Place South, Seattle, Washington, 98104. *Skiwear*

Edsbyn Sport Incorporated, 860 Decatur Avenue North, Minneapolis, Minnesota 55427. *Skis, boots, bindings, poles, accessories*

Elan-Monark, 208 Flynn Avenue, Burlington, Vermont 05401. *Skis*

Empire Ski Products, 22448 Statler Boulevard, St. Clair Shores, Michigan 48081. *Accessories*

Erik Sports Incorporated, P.O. Box 522, Saddle River, New Jersey 07458. *Skis, boots, bindings, poles*

Exel-Silenta Incorporated, 10-D Roessler Road, Woburn, Massachusetts 01801. *Skis, boots, bindings, poles, accessories, skiwear*

Fabiano Shoe Company Incorporated, 850 Summer Street, South Boston, Massachusetts 02127. *Boots*

Faering Design, Route 1, Box 223, Suttons Bay, Michigan 49682. *Accessories*

Fila Sports Incorporated, 831 Industrial Road, San Carols, California 94070. *Skiwear*

Fischer of America Incorporated, 35 Industrial Parkway, Woburn, Massachusetts 01801. *Skis, boots, bindings*

Fox River Mills Incorporated, P.O. Box 298, 227 Poplar Street, Osage, Iowa 50461. *Skiwear*

Fuji America, 1840 Northwestern Avenue, Gurnee, Illinois 60031. *Skis, boots, bindings, poles, accessories*

Gates-Mills Incorporated, Johnstown, New York 12059. *Skiwear*

The Grandoe Corporation, 72 Bleecker Street, Gloversville, New York 12078. *Skiwear*

Hagan Ski USA, 410 West Lombard Street, Baltimore, Maryland 21201. *Skis, boots, bindings, poles*

Hagemeister-Lert Incorporated, 345 Fourth Street, San Francisco, California 94107. *Skiwear*

Halstead Imports Incorporated, 3627 East 8th Street, P.O. Box 23458, Los Angeles, California 90023. *Skiwear*

Haugen Nordic, 1 Spencer Street, P.O. Box 708, Lebanon, New Hampshire 03766. *Skis, boots, bindings, poles, accessories*

Heierling of Switzerland Limited, 56 Maple Street, Warwick, Rhode Island 02888. *Boots*

Helly-Hansen Incorporated, 3848 148th Avenue Northeast, P.O. Box C-31, Redmond, Washington, 98052. *Skiwear*

Hertel & Company Incorporated, P.O. Box 10, Cupertino, California 95015. *Accessories*

Holley International Company, 63 Kercheval, Suite 204-A, Grosse Pointe Farms, Michigan 48236. *Accessories*

Jansport, Paine Field Industrial Park, Everett, Washington 98204. *Accessories*

Jarvinen USA, 47 Congress Street, P.O. Box 46, Salem, Massachusetts 01970. *Skis, boots, bindings, poles, accessories*

Karhu-Titan USA Incorporated, 55 Green Mountain Drive, South Burlington, Vermont 05401. *Skis, accessories, skiwear*

Kastle USA Incorporated, 85 Executive Boulevard, Elmsford, New York 10523. *Skis*

Kenko International Corporation, 8141 West I-70 Frontage Road North, Arvada, Colorado 80002. *Boots, bindings*

Kenyon Consumer Products, 200 Main Street, Kenyon, Rhode Island 02836. *Skiwear*

Kneissl Incorporated, P.O. Box 178, Ward Hill, Massachusetts 01830. *Skis, accessories, skiwear*

Kristin International Limited, Box F, East Main Street, Turin, New York 13473. *Skiwear*

Landav Design, 333 Southwest Park, Portland, Oregon 97205. *Skiwear*

Le Lasso, 4396 Pepsi Drive, San Diego, California 92111. *Accessories*

Life-Link International Incorporated, P.O. Box 2913, 1240 Huff Lane, Jackson Hole, Wyoming 83001. *Poles, accessories*

MSHO Sports, P.O. Box 286, Depot Road, Putney, Vermont 05346. *Skiwear*

Marker USA, 295 Chipeta Way, Salt Lake City, Utah 84110. *Bindings*

Marmot Mountain Works Limited, 331 South 13th Street, Grant Junction, Colorado 81501. *Skiwear*

Maxiglide Products Incorporated, P.O. Box 302, 131 West Beaver Avenue, State College, Pennsylvania 16801. *Accessories*

Merrell Boot Company, Denali International Incorporated, Route 1, Box 105, Waitsfield, Vermont 05673. *Boots, accessories*

Miller Ski Company, 1175 North 1200 West, Orem, Utah 84057. *Skis, boots, poles, accessories, skiwear*

Mother Karen's Ski and Sportswear, 3479 Southwest Temple, Salt Lake City, Utah 84115. *Skiwear*

Mother Lode Incorporated, 650 North Highway 169, Lorimor, Iowa 50149. *Skiwear*

Mountain Ladies & Ewe, Box 391, Manchester Village, Vermont 05254. *Skiwear*

Mountain Masters, 3030 Panorama, P.O. Box 1129, Tahoe City, California 95730. *Accessories, skiwear*

Mountainsmith, 12790 West 6th Place, Golden, Colorado 80401. *Accessories*

Mt. Tam Sports, Box 111, Kentfield, California 94914. *Skiwear*

Nike Incorporated, 3900 Southwest Murray Boulevard, Beaverton, Oregon 97005. *Boots*

Normark Corporation, 1200 East 79th Street, Bloomington, Minnesota 55420. *Skis, boots, bindings, poles*

Norski of America Limited, 1642 Doty Street, Oshkosh, Wisconsin 54901. *Skis, boots, bindings, poles, accessories*

North By Northeast, 181 Conant Street, Pawtucket, Rhode Island 02862. *Accessories, skiwear*

The North Face, 1234 Fifth Street, Berkeley, California 94710. *Skiwear*

Nortur Incorporated, 2000 East Center Circle, Minneapolis, Minnesota 55441. *Skis, boots, bindings, poles, accessories*

OU Sports Incorporated/Kazama International Limited, 1926 Third Avenue, Seattle, Washington 98101. *Skis*

Odlo USA, 69 North Main Street, Farmington, Maine 04938. *Skiwear*

Outdoor Products, 533 South Los Angeles Street, Los Angeles, California 90013. *Accessories, skiwear*

Outdoor Research, 17423 Beach Drive Northeast, Seattle, Washington 98155. *Accessories*

Patagonia Software, P.O. Box 150, Ventura, California 93002. *Skiwear*

Phillips Temro Incorporated, 9700 West 74th Street, Eden Prairie, Minnesota. *Accessories*

Phoenix Ski Company, 111 Baltic Avenue, Aspen, Colorado 81611. *Skis*

Piper Sport Racks Incorporated, 1161 Chess Drive, P.O. Box 4209, Foster City, California 94404. *Accessories*

Powderhorn Mountaineering Incorporated, 1777 Oakdale Avenue, P.O. Box 43438, St. Paul, Minnesota 55164. *Skiwear*

Protogs Incorporated, 1333 Broadway, New York, New York 10018. *Skiwear*

REI Co-op, P.O. Box C88126, Seattle, Washington 98188. *Accessories*

Rec Aids Company, P.O. Box 710, Schenectady, New York, 12801. *Accessories*

Reliable Racing Supply, 624 Glen Street, Glens Falls, New York 12801. *Skis, boots, poles, accessories*

Rossignol Ski Company Incorporated, Industrial Avenue, P.O. Box 298, Williston, Vermont 05495. *Skis*

Royal Optical Company Incorporated, 400 Mathew Street, Santa Clara, California 95050. *Accessories*

Royal Robbins Incorporated, 1314 Coldwell Avenue, Modesto, California 95330. *Skiwear*

Ruffolo Enterprises, 6201 22nd Avenue, Kenosha, Wisconsin 53140. *Accessories*

G.R. Ryder Company, 663 Linda Avenue Northeast, Salem, Oregon 97303. *Accessories*

Salomon/North America Incorporated, 7 Dearborn Road, Peabody, Massachusetts 01960. *Boots, bindings*

Saranac Glove Company, P.O. Box 786, Green Bay, Wisconsin 54305. *Skiwear*

Sepp Sport, 1805 Monroe Street, Madison, Wisconsin 53711. *Poles, accessories.*

Sierra Designs, 247 Fourth Street, Oakland, California 94607. *Skiwear*

Skea Limited, P.O. Drawer J, Vail, Colorado 81658. *Skiwear*

Skilom, Volvo of America Corporation, Recreational Products Division, Building A, 206 Pegasus Avenue, Rockleigh, New Jersey 07647. *Skis, boots, poles*

Ski Tech International Incorporated, P.O. Box R, Wakefield, Massachusetts 01880. *Accessories*

Ski Tote USA, 21025 Osborne Street, Canoga Park, California 91304. *Accessories*

Spalding, 50 Jonergin Drive, Swanton, Vermont 05488. *Skis*

Sunbuster, 15115 Northeast 90th, Redmond, Washington 98052. *Skiwear*

Swallow Ski USA Incorporated, 812 Market Street, Kirkland, Washington 98033. *Skis*

Swix Sport USA Incorporated, Tracy Road, Chelmsford, Massachusetts 01824. *Boots, bindings, poles, accessories*

Tabar Incorporated, 177 Greenwich Avenue, Stamford, Connecticut 06902. *Skiwear*

Tomic Golf & Ski Manufacturing Incorporated, 23102 Mariposa Avenue, Torrance, California 90502. *Poles*

Trak Incorporated, 187 Neck Road, Ward Hill, Massachusetts 01830. *Skis, boots, bindings, poles*

Tyrol USA, 50 Jonergin Drive, Swanton, Vermont 05488. *Boots, bindings, accessories*

Vasque Boots/Red Wing Shoe Company, 419 Bush Street, Red Wing, Minnesota 55066. *Boots*

Warm Ewe Company, Hardy Hill, Lebanon, New Hampshire 03766. *Skiwear*

Wasatch Mountaineering, 920 West South Temple, Salt Lake City, Utah 84104. *Bindings, accessories*

F.H. Wiessner Company, 159 Lakeside Avenue, Burlington, Vermont 05401. *Skis, boots, accessories, skiwear*

Wigwam Mills Incorporated, P.O. Box 818, Sheboygan, Wisconsin 53081. *Skiwear*

Wyoming Woolens, Box 3127, 1250 Huff Lane, Jackson Hole, Wyoming 83001. *Accessories, skiwear*

Yakima, The Wheels of Industry, 820 North Street, Arcata, California 95521. *Accessories*

Zinik Manufacturing Company, 1638 South Redwood Road, Salt Lake City, Utah 84104. *Skiwear*

INDEX

Boldface entries denote photograph or illustration.

110